YEAR IN SPORTS 2011

SCHOLASTIC INC.
NEW YORK · TORONTO · LONDON · AUCKLAND
SYDNEY · MEXICO CITY · NEW DELHI · HONG KONG

ISBN 978-0-545-23749-9

10 9 8 7 6 5 4 3 2 1   10 11 12 13 14

Printed in the U.S.A.   40
First printing, December 2010

Produced by Shoreline Publishing Group LLC

Due to the publication date, records, results, and statistics are current as of August 2010.

CONTENTS

INTRODUCTION

The perfect ending to a great World Cup: Spain wins its first championship.

You know the old saying "Nobody's perfect"? (You probably used it on your last spelling test, right?) Well, in sports, that's not necessarily true. In sports, you can be perfect. It happened in baseball in 2010, when two pitchers tossed perfect games (and one more nearly did). It happened in soccer, when Spain's goalie was perfect—with five straight scoreless games—while his teammates scored enough to win the World Cup. It happened in college football, when Alabama was a perfect 14–0 and won the national championship. And it happened at the Winter Olympics, when Canadian fans saw the perfect ending to the Vancouver Games as their home team won the coveted ice hockey gold medal.

Of course, "perfect" doesn't always come from statistics. Some people would say that it was a perfect result when the New Orleans Saints won the Super Bowl,

The Saints marched in to a stunning Super Bowl victory.

capping off a rebirth for a state and a region still recovering from hurricanes and floods. The epic tennis match at Wimbledon between a pair of unheralded players gave tennis a perfect shot in the arm. Chicago Blackhawks fans had the perfect end to their season (and to decades of frustration) as their team won the Stanley Cup for the first time since 1961.

Perfect or not, we've got all the bases covered in this book (along with the courts, the fields, the rinks, the tracks, and the courses!). Inside, you'll find all the winners—perfect and otherwise—in all your favorite sports (plus a few you might not have heard of—see page 178!).

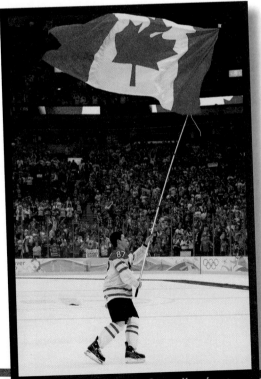

Sid the Kid became a Canadian hero.

You want heroes? We've got them all: Drew Brees and Peyton Manning; Kobe Bryant and Paul Pierce; Jonathan Toews and Sidney Crosby; Lindsey Vonn and Travis Pastrana; Jimmie Johnson and Jeff Gordon; Rafael Nadal and Serena Williams; Lorena Ochoa and Phil Mickelson. That's just a small handful of the stars you'll meet inside (look for their names in colored type!).

This is just the right book to thrill any sports fan. In fact . . . we think it's perfect!

TOP 10

MOMENTS IN SPORTS
8·2009 ▶ 8·2010

A perfect game. Any game that your favorite team wins is a perfect game, right?

From the Winter Olympics to the World Cup . . . from the Super Bowl to the NASCAR championship. There were perfect games in all sorts of sports in the past year. Once again, we're kicking off the *Scholastic Year in Sports* with a look at what we think were the top 10 moments or accomplishments of the past 12 months. There were an amazing number of special sports moments—perfect and otherwise—but can you guess which event was the number-one moment in the past year?

10   9   8

7 6 5 4 3 2...

10 It's not exactly a sport you can play in the backyard with your friends, but bobsledding has a long Olympic history. At the 2010 Winter Games, the U.S. four-man team, led by driver *Steve Holcomb*, captured the gold medal!

9 Other stock car drivers have won four titles, but only *Jimmie Johnson* has won four in a row. The California native snagged his fourth straight NASCAR championship in 2009.

8 On and on and on they played . . . for more than 11 hours . . . over 3 days . . . until finally *John Isner* (left) beat *Nicolas Mahut* at Wimbledon in the longest tennis match ever!

7 Chicago has long been a great hockey town, but it hadn't had a champion since 1961. Blackhawks captain *Jonathan Toews* and his mates took care of that and won the Stanley Cup in 2010.

6

For the first time in 130 years, there were two perfect games in one season. First, Oakland's *Dallas Braden* did it on May 9, then Phillies ace *Roy Halladay* followed on May 29.

5 Okay, so the United States lost. This was still a magical moment in sports, as Canada won the 2010 Olympic hockey gold while playing in Vancouver in front of delirious hometown fans.

4

*Celebrate! **Landon Donovan** raced for joy after scoring a dramatic last-moment goal to beat Algeria and send the United States forward to the Round of 16 in the World Cup.*

3 The faces tell the story. Detroit's *Armando Galarraga* could only smile as he walked away from the ump who stole his perfect game from him.

2 Lifting the spirits of an entire state and of anyone who loves Cinderella sports stories, *Terry Porter* of the Saints raced to the end zone with the touchdown that clinched a Super Bowl triumph for his team.

1 *The greatest joy in soccer: holding aloft the World Cup trophy. Spain captain and goalie **Iker Casillas** earned that honor with five shutouts, while his team played magical, marvelous soccer.*

MLB

GODZILLA SMASH!
Yankees designated hitter Hideki Matsui and Phillies catcher Carlos Ruiz watch with differing emotions as Matsui's home run flies into the night in Game 6 of the 2009 World Series. The two-run shot was part of a six-RBI night for the Japanese star, known back home as "Godzilla."

THEY DID IT AGAIN!

A-Rod (13) leads the Yanks in celebration!

Phils . . . New York won that one, too!

Something else that had been done before came in the postseason awards. **Albert Pujols** and **Tim Lincecum** both repeated their big NL awards: MVP and Cy Young, respectively. That was still pretty rare—there had not been a repeat MVP since **Barry Bonds** in 2004 or a repeat Cy Young since **Randy Johnson** in 2002. Pujols aimed for three straight with another outstanding season in 2010, while Lincecum got a lot of competition for the Cy Young from Colorado's **Ubaldo Jimenez** (see page 26). In the AL, **Joe Mauer** was making his own something new into something old. He won his first AL MVP award, but he also repeated as the batting champ. He became the first catcher with three league batting titles.

As 2010 began, some other things were happening again, including **Alex Rodriguez**'s continuing to smash homers. As 2010 rolled on, he set his sights on career homer number 600. With a blast in early August, he became only the seventh player to top that mark.

The last year in baseball was a mix of things that have happened before and things that had almost never happened.

Things that were not new: In 2009, the New York Yankees won their 27th World Series. No team in pro sports has won more championships than the Bronx Bombers. They had the best record in the majors in the regular season and kept it rolling in the play-offs. In the Series, they beat the NL-champion Phillies in six games, even as Philly became the first NL repeat champ since the 1975–76 Cincinnati Reds. Even the World Series was a repeat of the 1950 matchup between the Yanks and

Tim Lincecum was a strikeout king.

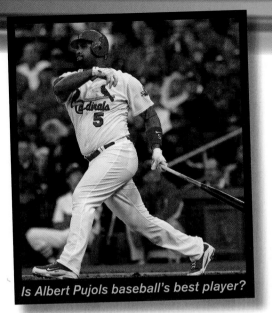

Is Albert Pujols baseball's best player?

What about those new things? The 2009 World Series MVP was **Hideki Matsui**, who became the first designated hitter AND first player born in Japan to earn that important honor. The 2010 season was the first since 1880 to include two perfect games (read more about them on pages 26–27). And for the first time, a pitcher lost a perfect game when an umpire made a bad call on what should have been the 27th out. Read **Armando Galarraga**'s amazing story on page 27. Finally, there was the awesome June 8 debut of Nationals pitcher **Stephen Strasburg**. Using a 100-mph heater, he blew away the Pirates, setting a strikeout record and the stage for a remarkable career (see page 30).

> **" Now we're winners. Rejoice! No one can take this away from the city of Philadelphia!"**
>
> — RYAN HOWARD

Pitching was a big story in other ways in 2010. Including the two perfectos, there were five no-hitters pitched in the major leagues, the most since 1990. Hitters couldn't wait for 2010 to be over!

2009 FINAL STANDINGS

AL EAST

Yankees	103–59
Red Sox	95–67
Rays	84–78
Blue Jays	75–87
Orioles	64–98

AL CENTRAL

Twins	87–76
Tigers	86–77
White Sox	79–83
Indians	65–97
Royals	65–97

AL WEST

Angels	97–65
Rangers	87–75
Mariners	85–77
Athletics	75–87

NL EAST

Phillies	93–86
Marlins	87–75
Braves	86–76
Mets	70–92
Nationals	59–103

NL CENTRAL

Cardinals	91–71
Cubs	83–78
Brewers	80–82
Reds	78–84
Astros	74–88
Pirates	62–99

NL WEST

Dodgers	95–67
Rockies	92–70
Giants	88–74
Padres	75–87
Diamondbacks	70–92

2009 AWARD WINNERS

MOST VALUABLE PLAYER

AL **Joe MAUER** ▶ ▶ ▶
MINNESOTA TWINS

NL **Albert PUJOLS**
ST. LOUIS CARDINALS

CY YOUNG AWARD

AL **Zack GREINKE**
KANSAS CITY ROYALS

NL **Tim LINCECUM**
SAN FRANCISCO GIANTS

ROOKIE OF THE YEAR

AL **Andrew BAILEY**
OAKLAND ATHLETICS

NL **Chris COGHLAN**
FLORIDA MARLINS

RELIEF PITCHER OF THE YEAR

AL **Joe NATHAN**
(TIE) MINNESOTA TWINS

Mariano RIVERA
NEW YORK YANKEES

NL **Heath BELL**
SAN DIEGO PADRES

MANAGER OF THE YEAR

AL **Mike SCIOSCIA**
LOS ANGELES ANGELS

NL **Jim TRACY**
COLORADO ROCKIES

HANK AARON AWARD
(Voted by fans as the top offensive
performers in each league)

AL **Derek JETER**
NEW YORK YANKEES

NL **Albert PUJOLS**
ST. LOUIS CARDINALS

ROBERTO CLEMENTE AWARD
(Given by Major League Baseball to honor
a player's work in the community)

Derek JETER
NEW YORK YANKEES

By the Numbers

2009 AL HITTING LEADERS

HOME RUNS: 39
Carlos PENA, RAYS

RBI: 122
Mark TEIXIERA, YANKEES

AVERAGE: .365
Joe MAUER, TWINS

STOLEN BASES: 70
Jacoby ELLSBURY, RED SOX

HITS: 225
Ichiro SUZUKI, MARINERS

2009 NL HITTING LEADERS

HOME RUNS: 47
Albert PUJOLS, CARDINALS

RBI: 141
Prince FIELDER, BREWERS ▶▶▶

AVERAGE: .342
Hanley RAMIREZ, MARLINS

STOLEN BASES: 61
Michael BOURN, ASTROS

HITS: 203
Ryan BRAUN, BREWERS

2009 AL PITCHING LEADERS

WINS: 19
Felix HERNANDEZ, MARINERS
C. C. SABATHIA, YANKEES
Justin VERLANDER, TIGERS

SAVES: 48
Brian FUENTES, ANGELS

ERA: 2.16
Zack GREINKE, ROYALS

STRIKEOUTS: 269
Justin VERLANDER, TIGERS

2009 NL PITCHING LEADERS

WINS: 19
Adam WAINWRIGHT, CARDINALS

SAVES: 42
Heath BELL, PADRES

ERA: 2.24
Chris CARPENTER, CARDINALS

STRIKEOUTS: 261
Tim LINCECUM, GIANTS

2009 POSTSEASON

AL DIVISION SERIES

Angels 3, Red Sox 0
The Halos used a two-out, two-run, ninth-inning rally to win Game 1, and went on to sweep the Sox.

Yankees 3, Twins 0
Alex Rodriguez busted out with a game-tying homer in Game 2. **Mark Teixiera** then whacked a walk off in the 11th to power a series sweep.

NL DIVISION SERIES

Dodgers 3, Cardinals 0
After the Dodgers won a sloppy Game 1 (the teams left 30 men on base!), they used a goof by **Matt Holliday** to win Game 2. **Vicente Padilla** shut down the Cards to complete the sweep.

Phillies 3, Rockies 1
Phillies ace **Cliff Lee** started his amazing postseason run with a big Game 1 win. The next three games were each decided by one run, but the Phillies won two of those to earn another trip to the NLCS.

AL CHAMPIONSHIP SERIES

Yankees 4, Angels 2
Three Angels errors helped **C. C. Sabathia** dominate in Game 1, while another error (and an A-Rod homer) gave the Yanks Game 2. Surprise hitting star **Jeff Mathis** hit a walk-off double to win Game 3 for the Angels. In Game 4, the umps blew several calls, but it was the Yankees' bats that did the most damage in a 10–1 win. The Yankees earned their 40th AL pennant by winning Game 6 behind play-off workhorse **Andy Pettitte**.

NL CHAMPIONSHIP SERIES

Phillies 4, Dodgers 1
A Dodgers team that was tops in the NL most of the season went quietly in the play-offs, losing to the defending champs. A Game 2 victory courtesy of a bases-loaded walk was the only bright spot for the Dodgers. For the Phillies, slugger **Ryan Howard** starred and earned the MVP nod, while **Jimmy Rollins** had a walk-off hit to win Game 4 and **Cliff Lee** kept mowin' hitters down. The Phillies became the first repeat NL champs since the 1976 Reds.

Cliff Lee led the Phillies to the NL title.

2009 WORLD SERIES

An action-packed World Series gave the Yanks their 27th crown. Check out the Series Notebook on page 29, too!

GAME 1
Phillies 6–Yankees 1

Chase Utley's first two homers of the series swamped Yankees ace **C. C. Sabathia**, while **Cliff Lee**'s nine innings of one-run ball proved too much for the Bombers.
WP: *Cliff Lee* **LP:** *C. C. Sabathia*
HR: *PHIL: Utley (2)*

GAME 2
Yankees 3–Phillies 1

A. J. Burnett righted the Yankees' ship, while homers from **Mark Teixiera** and **Hideki Matsui** gave the pitcher all the runs he needed in a 3–1 win.
WP: *A. J. Burnett*
LP: *Pedro Martinez*
HR: *NY: Teixiera, Matsui*

GAME 3
Yankees 8–Phillies 5

The Yankees shook off two homers from Philly outfielder **Jayson Werth** and got a big game from **A-Rod** to win, 8–5. A-Rod's homer was off a camera in right field! Yankees pitcher **Andy Pettitte** even chipped in with a key RBI single.
WP: *Andy Pettitte* **LP:** *Cole Hamels*
HR: *NY: Rodriguez, Swisher, Matsui; PHIL: Werth (2), Ruiz*

Matsui's big bat earned him a big MVP trophy.

GAME 4
Yankees 7–Phillies 4

A **Pedro Feliz** homer tied the score, 4–4, in the bottom of the eighth, but Phillies closer **Brad Lidge** gave up three runs in the ninth. **Mariano Rivera** shut down the Phillies (again!) to clinch a 7–4 win.
WP: *Joba Chamberlain*
LP: *Brad Lidge*
HR: *PHIL: Utley, Feliz*

GAME 5
Phillies 8–Yankees 6

Two more homers from **Utley**, including a three-run shot in the first inning, powered the Phillies to an 8–6 win. **Lee** struggled a bit on the mound, but the Philly offense finally got on track in a big way.
WP: *Lee*
LP: *Burnett*
HR: *PHIL: Utley (2), Ibanez*

GAME 6
Yankees 7–Phillies 3

Godzilla attacks Philadelphia! **Matsui** busted out with six RBI. That tied for most RBI ever in a World Series game, and powered the Yanks to their 27th championship.
WP: *Pettitte* **LP:** *Martinez*
HR: *Matsui*

WORLD SERIES MVP: DH HIDEKI MATSUI, Yankees—.615, 3 HR, 8 RBI

PITCHING PERFECTION!

Pitchers earned the biggest headlines in the 2010 season. Two of them joined an elite group of perfect-game pitchers. Another created a new sort of memory, one that was both sad and inspiring. Step up to the plate and see if you can handle the hot stuff these guys are throwing.

Braden's Best ▶

Perfect games are pretty rare. In more than 130 years and 300,000-plus big-league games, there had only been 18 before 2010. The most recent before this year was **Mark Buehrle**'s in 2009. And though they're rare, when you think of perfect games, you sort of expect that great pitchers might have one of them. **Sandy Koufax**, **Cy Young**, **Catfish Hunter** . . . all of them superstars.

And then there are the surprise pitchers who throw them. On May 9, 2010, **Dallas Braden** represented that group. The Oakland lefty was as unexpected a perfect-

game pitcher as anyone has ever been. He had a losing career record and was not known as a fireballing power pitcher. Yet he managed to baffle and fool the mighty Tampa Bay Rays, and won, 4–0. The Rays had the highest winning percentage of any team that had been "perfected."

A touching part of the story came after the game. Braden was raised by his grandmother after his mom died of cancer. So how cool was it that his grandmother was on hand for the Mother's Day game and shared a hug with Dallas afterward?

SUPER START

Amid all this great news about pitching, it's worth mentioning **Ubaldo Jimenez.** The hard-throwing Rockies righty threw a no-hitter on April 17. That was only part of one of the best first halves of pitching in decades. Through early August, Jimenez was 17–3 with a solid 2.55 ERA. He went 33 innings without giving up a run at one point. Keep an eye on this guy!

GALARRAGA'S GRACE

Believe it or not, yet another pitcher almost pitched a perfect game in 2010. On June 2, **Armando Galarraga** of Detroit set down 26 Cleveland Indians in a row. His team led, 3–0, so all that remained was to retire **Jason Donald**, who hit a grounder to first base. Galarraga ran to cover first, caught the ball, and stepped on first before Donald. Batter out . . . perfect game . . . right?

Wrong. First-base umpire **Jim Joyce**, to the shock of everyone in the ballpark, called Donald safe. Replays showed that Donald was clearly out, but replays don't count.

Galarraga could only shake his head and smile in disbelief. His chance at history was over with the blown call. He wrapped up the game with a win . . . and then things really got interesting.

How would you feel if someone made a mistake that snatched such a prize from you? And how would you feel if that person admitted the mistake, as Joyce did? It took a lot of courage for Joyce to admit that he had, as he said, "blown it for the kid." But the bigger news was what Galarraga did. He didn't get mad or upset. Instead, he earned nationwide praise for forgiving Joyce and hugging him the next day. The grace, poise, and sportsmanship of the two men made a bigger story than if Joyce had made the right call.

Halladay's Holiday! ▲

The only other time that there have been two perfect games in the same season was way back in 1880! **J. Lee Richmond** threw one for the old Worcester team, and five days later, **John Ward** tossed one for Providence. Move the calendar ahead 130 years, and welcome **Roy Halladay** to the history books. He threw a perfecto just 20 days after Braden did, making it only the second time there have been two in one season.

When Philly's Halladay did not allow a single Marlins base runner on May 29, 2010, it was stunning . . . but not surprising. Most players regard "Doc" as the best pitcher in the big leagues. He won the 2003 Cy Young Award and is a seven-time All-Star.

Against Florida, he was typically brilliant, striking out 11. He got help from third baseman **Juan Castro** on a couple of tough plays, too. He got the only run he needed in the 1–0 win thanks to a Marlins error. Halladay's biggest strength is his determination and focus. He never looked different or even smiled until the final out was called.

AROUND THE BASES

Too Much Celebration? ▶

Kendry Morales of the Angels got to live every player's dream in a game on May 29. He smacked a walk-off grand slam that gave his team a big win. His teammates gathered at home plate to greet him. He ran in, jumped in the air, and landed on home plate. Then his dream turned into a nightmare. He landed awkwardly and broke a bone in his lower leg! The fans' cheers went silent as they watched Morales get carried off on a stretcher. He had to miss most of the rest of the season . . . and the Angels made new rules to have calmer game-winning celebrations!

to Pittsburgh's **Nate McLouth** in April. He hit a walk-off homer to beat the Braves. As he rounded the bases, the entire Pittsburgh team ran out of the dugout . . . but not onto the field to celebrate. They ran into the clubhouse to hide! When McLouth got to home plate, no one was there to greet him, not even the batboy! When McLouth found his teammates in the locker room, they finally let him celebrate his big hit. Atlanta did the same thing to rookie **Jason Heyward** after his big Opening Day home run, too (page 30).

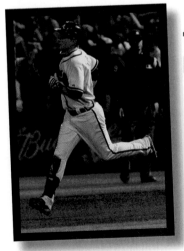

◀ Try This at Home!

Here's a little "inside baseball." When a young player does something really important in a key game, veteran teammates have a special way to tease him. It happened

Changes in the Classic

Baseball continued to tinker with the All-Star Game in 2010. To make sure that games don't end in ties and that managers have enough players, these new rules were put into place starting in 2010: Pitchers who throw for their teams on Sundays before the All-Star Game will be replaced on the All-Star roster. The DH will be used in all parks, not just AL ones. Rosters will now have 34 players. And the managers can choose one guy who can come back into the game even after he's left the lineup. Then the 2010 game was played, and fans saw the biggest change of all: The NL won! Their 3–1 victory at Angel Stadium was the first by the league since 1996.

2009 WORLD SERIES NOTEBOOK

* **Chase Utley** and **Babe Ruth** in the same sentence? The Phillies second baseman joined the Bambino as the only lefty batters in World Series history with a pair of homers off left-handed pitchers.

* In Game 1, **Cliff Lee** became the first pitcher since 1949 with 10 strikeouts and no walks in a Series game.

* **Alex Rodriguez** made history in Game 3. His shot to right field bounced off a camera atop the outfield wall. Umpires had to use video replay for the first time ever in a Series game to make the final call. ▶▶▶

* In Game 4, **Johnny Damon** stole two bases . . . on one play! After stealing second, he notice that no one was covering third base (due to a defensive shift), so he just kept running!

* With his fifth homer (which came in Game 5), **Chase Utley** tied the all-time record set by **Reggie "Mr. October" Jackson** for homers in one Series.

* **Hideki Matsui**'s six RBI in Game 6 tied a single-game record set by Yankees second baseman Bobby Richardson in a 1960 World Series game.

Great Starts!

It's one thing to have your major league dreams come true. What **Daniel Nava** did was beyond dreams. The young Red Sox outfielder hit the first pitch he ever faced in the big leagues for a grand slam! It was only the second time that has ever happened in baseball history.

Then Toronto catcher J. P. Arencibia did Nava one (or should we say two?) better. Arencibia blasted the first pitch he saw in the majors for a homer . . . and then he hit another in the same game! He went on to become the first player since 1900 with a pair of homers and a pair of doubles in his first big-league game! "What do I do next?" he asked afterward.

HELLO . . .

Several terrific young players made their debuts in 2010. Will they be the A-Rods and Roy Halladays of the future?

Jason HEYWARD, OF, ATLANTA ▶▶▶

Heyward wowed fans and opponents with his power. He was the first player under 21 years old with 16 RBI in his first dozen games since some guy named **Ted Williams**! By the All-Star break, he was among the NL leaders in RBI.

Mike LEAKE, P, CINCINNATI

Who needs the minors? Leake went from Arizona State directly to the Reds' rotation. He started out 5–0 with an ERA under 2.30.

Stephen STRASBURG, P, WASHINGTON

The most anticipated rookie debut in decades happened on June 8, when this 100-mph pitcher started his first big-league game. Amazingly, he topped all the hype. He became the first player EVER with 14 strikeouts and no walks in his MLB debut. Unfortunately, an August elbow injury might keep him off the mound for a year.

Mike STANTON, OF, FLORIDA

Is he the guy who strikes out a lot or the guy who hit 21 HRs in 53 minor-league games?

GOOD-BYE . . .

Each season, fans have to wave so long to many superstar players. Two players who came to fame in Seattle retired in 2010.

During spring training, **Randy Johnson**, "The Big Unit," decided to leave the mound for good. Johnson is considered one of the best lefties of all time. He won five Cy Young Awards. He led a league in strikeouts nine times, and is second all-time behind **Nolan Ryan** in career Ks. He also tossed a perfect game in 2004. He helped the Diamondbacks win the 2001 World Series and was the co-MVP.

◀◀◀ In June, **Ken Griffey Jr.** decided to hang up his cleats. "The Kid" is a surefire Hall of Famer, with 630 career homers and dozens of highlight-reel catches in center field. The winner of 10 Gold Gloves, the 1989 Rookie of the Year, and the 1997 AL MVP, Griffey won four AL home-run titles, too.

2010 HALL OF FAME

After a long flight, "The Hawk" finally landed in Cooperstown. **Andre Dawson** was elected in his ninth year of eligibility. A great all-around player for the Expos and Cubs, Dawson combined home-run power and base-stealing ability like few other players. And before his knees gave out on him, he was also one of the best outfielders of the 1980s, with a rocket for a right arm. He was a Rookie of the Year with Montreal in 1977 and the NL MVP with Chicago in 1987. He also won eight Gold Gloves and played in eight All-Star Games.

He was the only player elected this year, but he was joined at the Hall of Fame ceremony by new members **Whitey Herzog** and **Doug Harvey**. Herzog was the longtime manager of the Royals and Cardinals. He led St. Louis to three NL titles and the 1982 World Series championship. Harvey was a well-respected umpire. He was so sure of his calls that his nickname was simply "God."

Dawson combined power and speed.

2010 WORLD SERIES: A PREDICTION

Last year in this box, we said the Cardinals would win the 2009 World Series. Well, we were wrong about that one. But we're not defeated. Once again, because of printing deadlines, we don't know who won the 2010 World Series . . . but you might. See if we got it right this time! We gaze into the crystal baseball and say that the 2010 World Series champ is:

★Texas Rangers★

WORLD SERIES WINNERS

YEAR	WINNER	RUNNER-UP	SCORE*	YEAR	WINNER	RUNNER-UP	SCORE*
2009	New York Yankees	Philadelphia Phillies	4-2	1984	Detroit Tigers	San Diego Padres	4-1
2008	Philadelphia Phillies	Tampa Bay Rays	4-1	1983	Baltimore Orioles	Philadelphia Phillies	4-1
2007	Boston Red Sox	Colorado Rockies	4-0	1982	St. Louis Cardinals	Milwaukee Brewers	4-3
2006	St. Louis Cardinals	Detroit Tigers	4-1	1981	Los Angeles Dodgers	New York Yankees	4-2
2005	Chicago White Sox	Houston Astros	4-0	1980	Philadelphia Phillies	Kansas City Royals	4-2
2004	Boston Red Sox	St. Louis Cardinals	4-0	1979	Pittsburgh Pirates	Baltimore Orioles	4-3
2003	Florida Marlins	New York Yankees	4-2	1978	New York Yankees	Los Angeles Dodgers	4-2
2002	Anaheim Angels	San Francisco Giants	4-3	1977	New York Yankees	Los Angeles Dodgers	4-2
2001	Arizona Diamondbacks	New York Yankees	4-3	1976	Cincinnati Reds	New York Yankees	4-0
2000	New York Yankees	New York Mets	4-1	1975	Cincinnati Reds	Boston Red Sox	4-3
1999	New York Yankees	Atlanta Braves	4-0	1974	Oakland Athletics	Los Angeles Dodgers	4-1
1998	New York Yankees	San Diego Padres	4-0	1973	Oakland Athletics	New York Mets	4-3
1997	Florida Marlins	Cleveland Indians	4-3	1972	Oakland Athletics	Cincinnati Reds	4-3
1996	New York Yankees	Atlanta Braves	4-2	1971	Pittsburgh Pirates	Baltimore Orioles	4-3
1995	Atlanta Braves	Cleveland Indians	4-2	1970	Baltimore Orioles	Cincinnati Reds	4-1
1993	Toronto Blue Jays	Philadelphia Phillies	4-2	1969	New York Mets	Baltimore Orioles	4-1
1992	Toronto Blue Jays	Atlanta Braves	4-2	1968	Detroit Tigers	St. Louis Cardinals	4-3
1991	Minnesota Twins	Atlanta Braves	4-3	1967	St. Louis Cardinals	Boston Red Sox	4-3
1990	Cincinnati Reds	Oakland Athletics	4-0	1966	Baltimore Orioles	Los Angeles Dodgers	4-0
1989	Oakland Athletics	San Francisco Giants	4-0	1965	Los Angeles Dodgers	Minnesota Twins	4-3
1988	Los Angeles Dodgers	Oakland Athletics	4-1	1964	St. Louis Cardinals	New York Yankees	4-3
1987	Minnesota Twins	St. Louis Cardinals	4-3	1963	Los Angeles Dodgers	New York Yankees	4-0
1986	New York Mets	Boston Red Sox	4-3	1962	New York Yankees	San Francisco Giants	4-3
1985	Kansas City Royals	St. Louis Cardinals	4-3	1961	New York Yankees	Cincinnati Reds	4-1

YEAR	WINNER	RUNNER-UP	SCORE*	YEAR	WINNER	RUNNER-UP	SCORE*
1960	Pittsburgh Pirates	New York Yankees	4-3	1932	New York Yankees	Chicago Cubs	4-0
1959	Los Angeles Dodgers	Chicago White Sox	4-2	1931	St. Louis Cardinals	Philadelphia Athletics	4-3
1958	New York Yankees	Milwaukee Braves	4-3	1930	Philadelphia Athletics	St. Louis Cardinals	4-2
1957	Milwaukee Braves	New York Yankees	4-3	1929	Philadelphia Athletics	Chicago Cubs	4-1
1956	New York Yankees	Brooklyn Dodgers	4-3	1928	New York Yankees	St. Louis Cardinals	4-0
1955	Brooklyn Dodgers	New York Yankees	4-3	1927	New York Yankees	Pittsburgh Pirates	4-0
1954	New York Giants	Cleveland Indians	4-0	1926	St. Louis Cardinals	New York Yankees	4-3
1953	New York Yankees	Brooklyn Dodgers	4-2	1925	Pittsburgh Pirates	Washington Senators	4-3
1952	New York Yankees	Brooklyn Dodgers	4-3	1924	Washington Senators	New York Giants	4-3
1951	New York Yankees	New York Giants	4-2	1923	New York Yankees	New York Giants	4-2
1950	New York Yankees	Philadelphia Phillies	4-0	1922	New York Giants	New York Yankees	4-0
1949	New York Yankees	Brooklyn Dodgers	4-1	1921	New York Giants	New York Yankees	5-3
1948	Cleveland Indians	Boston Braves	4-2	1920	Cleveland Indians	Brooklyn Dodgers	5-2
1947	New York Yankees	Brooklyn Dodgers	4-3	1919	Cincinnati Reds	Chicago White Sox	5-3
1946	St. Louis Cardinals	Boston Red Sox	4-3	1918	Boston Red Sox	Chicago Cubs	4-2
1945	Detroit Tigers	Chicago Cubs	4-3	1917	Chicago White Sox	New York Giants	4-2
1944	St. Louis Cardinals	St. Louis Browns	4-2	1916	Boston Red Sox	Brooklyn Dodgers	4-1
1943	New York Yankees	St. Louis Cardinals	4-1	1915	Boston Red Sox	Philadelphia Phillies	4-1
1942	St. Louis Cardinals	New York Yankees	4-1	1914	Boston Braves	Philadelphia Athletics	4-0
1941	New York Yankees	Brooklyn Dodgers	4-1	1913	Philadelphia Athletics	New York Giants	4-1
1940	Cincinnati Reds	Detroit Tigers	4-3	1912	Boston Red Sox	New York Giants	4-3
1939	New York Yankees	Cincinnati Reds	4-0	1911	Philadelphia Athletics	New York Giants	4-2
1938	New York Yankees	Chicago Cubs	4-0	1910	Philadelphia Athletics	Chicago Cubs	4-1
1937	New York Yankees	New York Giants	4-1	1909	Pittsburgh Pirates	Detroit Tigers	4-3
1936	New York Yankees	New York Giants	4-2	1908	Chicago Cubs	Detroit Tigers	4-1
1935	Detroit Tigers	Chicago Cubs	4-2	1907	Chicago Cubs	Detroit Tigers	4-0
1934	St. Louis Cardinals	Detroit Tigers	4-3	1906	Chicago White Sox	Chicago Cubs	4-2
1933	New York Giants	Washington Senators	4-1	1905	New York Giants	Philadelphia Athletics	4-1

* Score is represented in games played.

SUPER SAINTS!

Tracy Porter races to the end zone with the interception that clinched a surprise Super Bowl win for the New Orleans Saints. The Saints beat the Indianapolis Colts, 31–17, for the first championship in team history.

NFL

PASSES NEVER FAIL!

The NFL has been around for almost a century, and for most of that time, running the ball was the number-one way to get around the field. Passing has always been a part of football, but to win games, you had to run the ball often and well. However, the 2009 season marked a big change—and one that might just be here to stay. Quarterbacks went nuts in 2009, setting dozens of records. There were 10 passers with more than 4,000 yards each, the most ever. Twelve QBs topped 25 touchdown passes, another all-time mark.

In the 90-year history of the NFL, only six quarterbacks have topped 4,000 yards and completed 68 percent of their passes in one season—THREE of them did it in 2009!

One thing that you just would not want to be in the NFL today: a defensive back!

There were more footballs flying around NFL stadiums than there are ducks in a winter migration. In a surprise, the Texans' **Matt Schaub** led the NFL with 4,770 passing yards, and he was followed closely by stars such as the Colts' **Peyton Manning**, the Saints' **Drew Brees**, and the Chargers' **Philip Rivers**. Even the Steelers, who usually run more than pass, took to the air: **Ben Roethlisberger** became the first Pittsburgh quarterback ever to top 4,000 yards.

Not surprisingly, with all the footballs being thrown about, receivers put up some pretty hefty numbers, too. The Texans' **Andre Johnson** became only the second player ever with back-to-back 1,500-yard-receiving seasons. Patriots wideout **Wes Welker**'s 123 catches for the season equaled the second-most ever. Broncos receiver **Brandon Marshall**'s 21 catches in one game were the most ever.

Strangely, amid all this fancy passing, one amazing running back showed that carryin' the rock might still be useful after all. **Chris Johnson** of the Titans became only the sixth player in NFL history to run for 2,000 yards in a season. He made it to 2,006 yards during the team's

Chris Johnson was a record-setting exception.

final game of the year. Other top runners included **Adrian Peterson** of the Vikings, who led the league with 18 rushing touchdowns, and the Jaguars' small but mighty **Maurice Jones-Drew**, who had 15 scores.

Of course, it all came down to power passing. The Super Bowl (see page 44) matched the Hall-of-Fame power of Manning with the Cinderella story of Brees and the Saints. In the end, the Saints prevailed to win their first championship, thrilling their long-suffering fans. Brees was named the game's MVP after—as you could have guessed—another spectacular passing performance.

2009 passing leader Matt Schaub

Final 2009 Regular-Season Standings

AFC EAST	W	L	NFC EAST	W	L
New England	10	6	Dallas	11	5
N.Y. Jets	9	7	Philadelphia	11	5
Miami	7	9	N.Y. Giants	8	8
Buffalo	6	10	Washington	4	12
AFC NORTH	**W**	**L**	**NFC NORTH**	**W**	**L**
Cincinnati	10	6	Minnesota	12	4
Baltimore	9	7	Green Bay	11	5
Pittsburgh	9	7	Chicago	7	9
Cleveland	5	11	Detroit	2	14
AFC SOUTH	**W**	**L**	**NFC SOUTH**	**W**	**L**
Indianapolis	14	2	New Orleans	13	3
Houston	9	7	Atlanta	9	7
Tennessee	8	8	Carolina	8	8
Jacksonville	7	9	Tampa Bay	3	13
AFC WEST	**W**	**L**	**NFC WEST**	**W**	**L**
San Diego	13	3	Arizona	10	6
Denver	8	8	San Francisco	8	8
Oakland	5	11	Seattle	5	11
Kansas City	4	12	St. Louis	1	15

THE 2009 POSTSEASON

Here's how the road to Super Bowl XLIV went. (Home teams are listed in capital letters.)

Karlos Dansby clinched Arizona's play-off win.

Wild-Card Weekend

AFC **N.Y. Jets 24, CINCINNATI 14**
Baltimore 33, NEW ENGLAND 14

NFC **DALLAS 34, Philadelphia 14**
ARIZONA 51, Green Bay 45 (OT)

Divisional Play-offs

AFC **INDIANAPOLIS 20, Baltimore 3**
N.Y. Jets 17, SAN DIEGO 14

NFC **NEW ORLEANS 45, Arizona 14**
MINNESOTA 34, Dallas 3

Conference Championships

AFC **INDIANAPOLIS 30, N.Y. Jets 17**
NFC **NEW ORLEANS 31, Minnesota 28 (OT)**

Super Bowl XLIV

New Orleans 31, Indianapolis 17

AWARD WINNERS

NFL MVP: PEYTON MANNING, QB, Colts

OFFENSIVE PLAYER OF THE YEAR: CHRIS JOHNSON, RB, Titans

DEFENSIVE PLAYER OF THE YEAR: CHARLES WOODSON, CB, Packers

OFFENSIVE ROOKIE OF THE YEAR: PERCY HARVIN, WR, Vikings

DEFENSIVE ROOKIE OF THE YEAR: BRIAN CUSHING, LB, Texans

WALTER PAYTON NFL MAN OF THE YEAR: BRIAN WATERS, G, Chiefs

All-Decade Team

At the end of the 2009 season, these players were named the NFL's best of the decade by a special Pro Football Hall of Fame selection committee:

OFFENSE

QUARTERBACKS: **Tom BRADY, Peyton MANNING**

RUNNING BACKS: **Shaun ALEXANDER, Edgerrin JAMES, Jamal LEWIS, LaDainian TOMLINSON**

FULLBACK: **Lorenzo NEAL**

WIDE RECEIVERS: **Marvin HARRISON, Torry HOLT, Randy MOSS, Terrell OWENS**

TIGHT ENDS: **Antonio GATES, Tony GONZALEZ**

TACKLES: **Walter JONES, Jonathan OGDEN, Orlando PACE, William ROAF**

GUARDS: **Larry ALLEN, Alan FANECA, Steve HUTCHINSON, Will SHIELDS**

CENTERS: **Olin KREUTZ, Kevin MAWAE**

DEFENSE

ENDS: **Dwight FREENEY, Julius PEPPERS, Michael STRAHAN, Jason TAYLOR**

TACKLES: **La'Roi GLOVER, Warren SAPP, Richard SEYMOUR, Kevin WILLIAMS**

LINEBACKERS: **Derrick BROOKS, Ray LEWIS, Joey PORTER, Zach THOMAS, Brian URLACHER, DeMarcus WARE**

CORNERBACKS: **Champ BAILEY, Ronde BARBER, Ty LAW, Charles WOODSON**

SAFETIES: **Brian DAWKINS, Troy POLAMALU, Ed REED, Darren SHARPER**

SPECIAL TEAMS

KICKERS: **David AKERS, Adam VINATIERI**

PUNTERS: **Shane LECHLER, Brian MOORMAN**

KICK RETURNERS: **Joshua CRIBBS, Dante HALL**

PUNT RETURNERS: **Dante HALL, Devin HESTER**

THE LEADERS

The top performers in some key NFL statistical categories for 2009:

2,006 RUSHING YARDS
Chris Johnson, Tennessee

109.6 PASSER RATING
Drew Brees, New Orleans

123 RECEPTIONS
Wes Welker, New England

146 POINTS
Nate Kaeding, San Diego

18 TOUCHDOWNS
Adrian Peterson, Minnesota

◀◀◀**17** SACKS **Elvis Dumervil**, Denver

9 INTERCEPTIONS **Jairus Byrd**, Buffalo; **Asante Samuel**, Philadelphia; **Darren Sharper**, New Orleans; **Darren Woodson**, Green Bay

32 FIELD GOALS **David Akers**, Philadelphia; **Nate Kaeding**, San Diego

51.1 PUNTING YARDS **Shane Lechler**, Oakland

29.1 KICKOFF RETURN YARDS **Clifton Smith**, Tampa Bay

15.2 PUNT RETURN YARDS **DeSean Jackson**, Philadelphia

These players set NFL records or reached key milestones in 2009:

Miles Austin, WR, Dallas

The Cowboys were hurting at wide receiver, so they gave the fourth-year player his first starting assignment. Result: a club-record 250 receiving yards, including the game-winning catch in overtime against Kansas City.

John Carney, K, New Orleans;
Matt Stover, K, Indianapolis

They became the fourth and fifth players in NFL history to score 2,000 career points.

Fred Jackson, RB, Buffalo

He became the first player in NFL history to rush for more than 1,000 yards and return kicks for more than 1,000 yards in the same season.

Chris Johnson, RB, Tennessee

With 2,006 yards rushing, he became just the sixth player—and the first since 2003—to top 2,000 yards in a season. He also caught 50 passes for 503 yards to give him an NFL-record 2,509 yards from scrimmage for the season.

Peyton Manning, QB, Indianapolis

He became the fourth passer to top 50,000 yards passing for his career. **Dan Marino**, **John Elway**, and **Brett Favre** got there before him.

Brandon Marshall, WR, Denver

He set an NFL record by catching an amazing 21 passes in a single game against the Colts. Only problem: Indianapolis still won!

Adrian Peterson, RB, Minnesota ▶▶▶

He joined some elite company by rushing for more than 1,300 yards (he had 1,383) and 10 touchdowns (he had 18) for the third time in his three NFL seasons. The only other players to begin a career that way: Pro Football Hall of Famers **Earl Campbell** and **Barry Sanders**.

Ben Roethlisberger, QB, Pittsburgh

In a wild win over Green Bay, "Big Ben" became just the 10th NFL quarterback ever to pass for 500 yards (he had 503) in a game.

Darren Sharper, S, New Orleans

He returned interceptions 97 yards and 99 yards for touchdowns. The only other player ever with two 90-plus-yard returns in the same season: Deion Sanders.

10 GREAT GAMES

There were so many great games in 2009 that Super Bowl XLIV doesn't even make this list! That was a pretty good game, though. (See page 44.)

#3: *An odd call by the Patriots led to a game-winning TD from Reggie Wayne.*

1 NEW ORLEANS 31, MINNESOTA 28
(NFC Championship Game, overtime)

The Saints booked a trip to the Super Bowl when **Garrett Hartley** kicked a 40-yard field goal in overtime. New Orleans was in danger of losing until **Tracy Porter** intercepted a pass in the final minute of the fourth quarter.

2 ARIZONA 51, GREEN BAY 45
(NFC Wild-Card Game, overtime)

The Cardinals' **Kurt Warner** passed for five TDs, and the Packers' **Aaron Rodgers** passed for four, but a defensive play—**Karlos Dansby's** 17-yard fumble return—ended the highest-scoring play-off game ever.

3 INDIANAPOLIS 35, NEW ENGLAND 34 (Week 10)

After the Patriots failed on a stunning fourth-and-2 try in their own territory late in the game (see page 46), the Colts won it on **Peyton Manning**'s 1-yard touchdown pass to **Reggie Wayne** with 13 seconds to go.

4 PITTSBURGH 37, GREEN BAY 36
(Week 15)

The defending NFL champs won with a play that looked a lot like their game winner in Super Bowl XLIII. **Ben Roethlisberger** tossed a 19-yard TD pass to **Mike Wallace** as time ran out.

5 DETROIT 38, CLEVELAND 37 ▶▶▶
(Week 11)

Both teams were 1–8 going in, but they played one of the most thrilling games of the season.

#6: No place like somebody else's home: Tynes's field goal beat the Cowboys.

Lions rookie **Matthew Stafford** passed for five TDs, including the winning 1-yarder on the last play.

6 N.Y. GIANTS 33, DALLAS 31
(Week 2)

The Giants won the first regular-season game in the Cowboys' $1.15 billion stadium before more than 105,000 fans. **Lawrence Tynes** won it on a 37-yard field goal with no time left.

7 TENNESSEE 20, ARIZONA 17
(Week 12)

The Titans drove 99 yards in the final 2:37 to pull out a comeback victory. The winning points came on **Vince Young**'s 10-yard touchdown pass to **Kenny Britt** as time ran out.

8 MIAMI 31, N.Y. JETS 27 (Week 5)

The lead changed hands five times in the fourth quarter of this game. The last time came on **Ronnie Brown**'s winning 2-yard run from the "Wildcat" formation with six seconds left.

9 MINNESOTA 30, GREEN BAY 23
(Week 4)

This was quarterback **Brett Favre**'s return to Green Bay. The Packers legend passed for three touchdowns to lead the Vikings over his former team.

10 NEW ENGLAND 25, BUFFALO 24
(Week 1)

The Patriots pulled out a dramatic win by scoring two touchdowns in the final 2:06. Both came on passes from quarterback **Tom Brady**. It was Brady's first game back since he had knee surgery following an injury he suffered in the first game of the 2008 season. His solid return let New England fans breathe a sigh of relief.

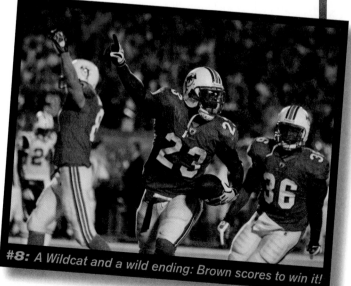

#8: A Wildcat and a wild ending: Brown scores to win it!

SURPRISE! SAINTS WIN!

Talk about a feel-good story. Just a few years ago, the New Orleans Saints' home in the Superdome was surrounded by floodwaters from Hurricane Katrina and filled with desperate people fleeing the storm. The team and its players helped with the rebuilding right afterward. In February 2010, they helped the city come all the way back. By winning Super Bowl XLIV, the Saints proved to be the city's saviors.

The game itself, against the Indianapolis Colts, was terrific. Fans were still buzzing about the halftime show when **Thomas Morstead** got ready to kick off to start the third quarter. At the time, the Colts were leading, 10–6, thanks to a TD pass from **Peyton Manning** to **Pierre Garcon**.

Brees proudly hoists the Super Bowl trophy.

"Four years ago, who ever thought this would be happening when 85 percent of the city was underwater? " — SAINTS QUARTERBACK DREW BREES

Morstead approached the ball as usual, but instead of kicking deep, he squibbed the ball toward the left sideline. Surprise! It was an onside kick.

An onside kick is rarely successful. It's usually only tried when a team is behind late in the game, and the other team knows it's coming. But in this case, Indianapolis did not expect it, and it turned out to be the play that sparked the Saints to a 31–17 victory and the first championship in their 43-year history.

Morstead's kick bounced off receiver **Hank Baskett**'s hands and, after uncovering a huge pile of players, officials determined that the Saints' **Chris Reis** had recovered the ball. It was the first onside kick used before the fourth quarter in Super Bowl history. Six plays later, quarterback **Drew Brees** tossed a 16-yard touchdown pass to running back **Pierre Thomas**, and New Orleans had the lead for the first time.

The Colts weren't going to go down without a fight, and they regained the lead at 17–13 when **Joseph Addai** ran 4 yards for a touchdown midway through the third quarter. The Saints countered with a field goal on their next drive, and then with Brees's 2-yard touchdown pass to tight end **Jeremy Shockey** on their next possession after that. A two-point conversion pass put New Orleans ahead 24–17 with 5:42 left.

One of the biggest plays was this onside kick recovery by the Saints to start the second half.

The Colts had plenty of time for a tying touchdown, and they marched from their 30-yard line to the Saints' 31 with 3:29 remaining. Manning looked to his left and fired in the direction of **Reggie Wayne**, his go-to receiver.

As soon as Manning let go of the ball, he knew it was a bad idea. Saints cornerback **Tracy Porter** recognized the play, and he jumped the route. He intercepted the pass and took off in the opposite direction. Seventy-four yards later, Porter crossed the goal line and set off a celebration in New Orleans.

Brees was named the game's Most Valuable Player after completing 32 of 39 passes for 288 yards and two touchdowns.

Wide receivers **Marques Colston** and **Devery Henderson** each had seven catches for the Saints.

Manning completed 31 of 45 passes for 333 yards for the Colts, but it wasn't enough. Making all the fans in their "Who Dat?" fan club thrilled beyond words, the Saints went marching in . . . to the Super Bowl championship.

BOX SCORE

New Orleans	0	6	10	15	—	31
Indianapolis	10	0	7	0	—	17

Ind–FG Stover 38
Ind–Garcon 19 pass from Manning (Stover kick)
NO–FG Hartley 46
NO–FG Hartley 44
NO–Thomas 16 pass from Brees (Hartley kick)
Ind–Addai 4 run (Stover kick)
NO–FG Hartley 47
NO–Shockey 2 pass from Brees (Moore pass from Brees)
NO–Porter 74 interception return (Hartley kick)

SIDELINE STORIES

You Make the Call

It's fourth down and 2 yards to go. You have the ball on your own 28-yard line, and your team is leading, 34–28, with just over two minutes to play. What do you do? Punt, of course!

Well, not necessarily, said Patriots coach **Bill Belichick**. In just that situation against the undefeated Colts in week 10 of 2009, Belichick had his team go for it. The play fell short of a first down, Indianapolis got the ball back, and the Colts drove to the winning touchdown in the final seconds. Indy won, 35–34.

◀◀◀ Helping Hands

You could certainly excuse Colts wide receiver **Pierre Garcon** if his mind was elsewhere during the NFL postseason in January and February of 2010. Garcon was born in Florida, but his parents are Haitian. Many of his family and friends were affected by the devastating earthquake that struck on January 12, 2010. So Garcon had added motivation to do his best in the AFC Championship Game in January. He

Fantasy Stars

All that passing in the NFL (see page 36) made quarterbacks the big stars in fantasy football in 2009. Winning fantasy owners almost always had to have a player like **Drew Brees**, **Peyton Manning**, **Aaron Rodgers**, or **Matt Schaub** on their team. Or, then again, maybe they just had to have one amazing running back: the Titans' **Chris Johnson**. He was a one-man fantasy team last year, when he totaled more yards from scrimmage in one season than any other player in NFL history. Add in his 16 TDs and he put together a giant package of points for his fantasy owners.

set a conference championship game record by catching 11 passes in the Colts' victory over the Jets for the AFC title. After the game, Garcon carried a Haitian flag on the victory platform. Garcon was among many NFL players who helped raise money after the quake.

Quick Thinking

Here's a play that football coaches and fellow players loved—and fantasy owners hated! The Jacksonville Jaguars were trailing the New York Jets, 22–21, late in their game at the Meadowlands, New Jersey, in week 10. Jaguars running back **Maurice Jones-Drew** took a handoff from the 10-yard line and had a clear path to the end zone. He got to the 1-yard line . . . and took a knee. Drew didn't want to score a touchdown and give the Jets a chance to still win the game. Instead, his heads-up play let Jacksonville run down the clock to only a few seconds left. Then **Josh Scobee** kicked a 21-yard field goal as time ran out, for a 24–22 victory.

He Could Go All the Way!

Cleveland kickoff returner **Joshua Cribbs** went a long way to get into the record books. He entered Cleveland's game at Kansas City in week 15 tied with several players for the most career kickoff-return touchdowns in NFL history, with six. In the first quarter, Cribbs broke the record

CAPTAIN KURT RETIRES

From stocking shelves at the supermarket to a probable spot in the Pro Football Hall of Fame one day, quarterback **Kurt Warner** had a storybook football journey. The two-time NFL MVP and former Super Bowl MVP retired at the top of his game in 2009, when he passed for 3,753 yards and 26 touchdowns while leading the Cardinals to the play-offs. Warner, who worked in a grocery store to pay the bills while trying to make it in football, played 12 NFL seasons. He passed for a total of 32,344 yards and 208 touchdowns.

◀◀◀ 32 for No. 4

Brett Favre completed a unique feat in 2009: He became the first quarterback to win starts against each of the NFL's 32 teams during his career. The last team on Favre's checklist was the Green Bay Packers, the team for which he played from 1992 through 2007. In week 4 of 2009, Favre's most recent team, the Minnesota Vikings, beat Green Bay in a raucous Monday-night game at the Metrodome, 30–23.

Almost Perfect

The unique distinction of the 1972 Miami Dolphins is safe for at least another year. That team, which won Super Bowl VII, remains the only undefeated and untied team (through the regular season and the postseason) in NFL history. Both the Indianapolis Colts and the New Orleans Saints made a run at perfection in 2009. In fact, it was the first time that two teams started out with 13 wins in the same year. The Colts' streak eventually reached 14 games before they were beaten by the New York Jets in a game in which Indianapolis rested its starters for much of the second half. New Orleans's run ended with a loss to Dallas in game 14. The Saints didn't win again in the regular season—but things turned out pretty well for them in the end!

when he raced 100 yards for a touchdown on the kickoff. He wasn't done, though. In the second quarter, Cribbs took another kickoff 103 yards for a score.

59–0!

That was the unbelievable score when the Patriots beat the Titans in a historic rout. The Patriots led, 10–0, after the opening 15 minutes, then blitzed Tennessee for 35 points in the second period. They reached 59 points in the third quarter . . . and didn't even have to score in the fourth! New England's win was the NFL's biggest rout since 1970. (The all-time record? Bears 73–Redskins 0 in 1940!)

CLASS OF 2010

If there was such a thing as a Hall of Fame of Hall of Famers, **Jerry Rice** and **Emmitt Smith** surely would be in it! Rice is the NFL's all-time leading pass catcher and he scored more touchdowns than any other player. He also made the Pro Bowl 13 times in 20 NFL seasons. Smith is the league's all-time leading rusher. He was an all-star 8 times in his first 10 seasons. It was no surprise, then, that both Rice and Smith were voted into the Pro Football Hall of Fame in 2010, in their first year of eligibility. Here's the entire Hall of Fame Class of 2010:

WHO'S NEXT

There aren't any sure things for induction into the Hall of Fame in 2011. But there are a few guys who have a pretty good chance of making it in the first year they are eligible. (Players have to be retired for five seasons before they can be elected.) Among them: former shutdown cornerback and star punt returner **Deion Sanders**, running backs **Marshall Faulk** and **Curtis Martin**, and tackle **Willie Roaf**.

Russ Grimm, G
Washington (1981–1991)

Rickey Jackson, LB
New Orleans (1981–1993),
San Francisco (1994–95)

Dick LeBeau, CB
Detroit (1959–1972)

Floyd Little, RB
Denver (1967–1975)

John Randle, DT
Minnesota (1990–2000),
Seattle (2001–03)

Jerry Rice, WR
San Francisco (1985–2000),
Oakland (2001–04), Seattle (2004)

◄◄◄ Emmitt Smith, RB
Dallas (1990–2002), Arizona (2003–04)

TOMORROW'S LEGENDS TODAY

The young guys on this page—they were all in their first or second year in 2009—aren't in the same class as the all-time greats on the previous page. Not yet, anyway! They could be one day, though, after the terrific start they've had to their NFL careers.

PERCY HARVIN, WR, MINNESOTA

He ran, caught passes, and returned kicks for a combined total of 2,081 yards in his rookie season in 2009.

DESEAN JACKSON, WR, PHILADELPHIA

Jackson is a big play waiting to happen. He scored 12 touchdowns in 2009, and 8 of them covered 50 or more yards.

CHRIS JOHNSON, RB, HOUSTON

Two years. Two Pro Bowls. Two steps closer to Canton. (That's where the Hall of Fame is!)

BRIAN ORAKPO, LB, WASHINGTON ▶▶▶

He was a defensive end in college who had no trouble making the move to outside linebacker in the pros. He had 11 sacks as a rookie.

RAY RICE, RB, BALTIMORE

There may be no better rushing-receiving threat in the NFL right now than Rice—well, except for that **Chris Johnson** guy.

MARK SANCHEZ, QB, NEW YORK JETS

The Jets traded up to pick him in 2009, and he helped lead them all the way to the AFC Championship Game.

NEW FOR 2010

CHOICE	PLAYER	POSITION	TEAM
1.	Sam Bradford	QB	Rams
2.	Ndamukong Suh	DT	Lions
3.	Gerald McCoy	DT	Buccaneers
4.	Trent Williams	T	Redskins
5.	Eric Berry	S	Chiefs
6.	Russell Okung	T	Seahawks
7.	Joe Haden	CB	Browns
8.	Rolando McClain	LB	Raiders
9.	C.J. Spiller	RB	Bills
10.	Tyson Alualu	DE	Jaguars
11.	Anthony Davis	T	49ers
12.	Ryan Mathews	RB	Chargers
13.	Brandon Graham	DE	Eagles
14.	Earl Thomas	S	Seahawks
15.	Jason Pierre-Paul	DE	Giants
16.	Derrick Morgan	DE	Titans
17.	Mike Iupati	G	49ers
18.	Maurkice Pouncey	C	Steelers
19.	Sean Weatherspoon	LB	Falcons
20.	Kareem Jackson	CB	Texans
21.	Jermaine Gresham	TE	Bengals
22.	Demaryius Thomas	WR	Broncos
23.	Bryan Bulaga	T	Packers
24.	Dez Bryant	WR	Cowboys
25.	Tim Tebow	QB	Broncos
26.	Dan Williams	DT	Cardinals
27.	Devin McCourty	CB	Patriots
28.	Jared Odrick	DT	Dolphins
29.	Kyle Wilson	CB	Jets
30.	Jahvid Best	RB	Lions
31.	Jerry Hughes	DE	Colts
32.	Patrick Robinson	CB	Saints

For the eighth time in the decade of the 2000s, a quarterback was the first overall pick in the NFL Draft. This time around, it was **Sam Bradford** from Oklahoma. He was chosen by the St. Louis Rams. He was followed by a couple of powerful defensive tackles: **Ndamukong Suh** and **Gerald McCoy**. Six of the top ten picks were on defense!

FOR THE RECORD

Super Bowl Winners

GAME	SEASON	WINNING TEAM	LOSING TEAM	SCORE	SITE
I	1966	**Green Bay**	Kansas City	**35–10**	Los Angeles
II	1967	**Green Bay**	Oakland	**33–14**	Miami
III	1968	**N.Y. Jets**	Baltimore	**16–7**	Miami
IV	1969	**Kansas City**	Minnesota	**23–7**	New Orleans
V	1970	**Baltimore**	Dallas	**16–13**	Miami
VI	1971	**Dallas**	Miami	**24–3**	New Orleans
VII	1972	**Miami**	Washington	**14–7**	Los Angeles
VIII	1973	**Miami**	Minnesota	**24–7**	Houston
IX	1974	**Pittsburgh**	Minnesota	**16–6**	New Orleans
X	1975	**Pittsburgh**	Dallas	**21–17**	Miami
XI	1976	**Oakland**	Minnesota	**32–14**	Pasadena
XII	1977	**Dallas**	Denver	**27–10**	New Orleans
XIII	1978	**Pittsburgh**	Dallas	**35–31**	Miami
XIV	1979	**Pittsburgh**	Los Angeles	**31–19**	Pasadena
XV	1980	**Oakland**	Philadelphia	**27–10**	New Orleans
XVI	1981	**San Francisco**	Cincinnati	**26–21**	Pontiac, Mich.
XVII	1982	**Washington**	Miami	**27–17**	Pasadena
XVIII	1983	**L.A. Raiders**	Washington	**38–9**	Tampa
XIX	1984	**San Francisco**	Miami	**38–16**	Stanford
XX	1985	**Chicago**	New England	**46–10**	New Orleans

GAME	SEASON	WINNING TEAM	LOSING TEAM	SCORE	SITE
XXI	1986	**N.Y. Giants**	Denver	**39–20**	Pasadena
XXII	1987	**Washington**	Denver	**42–10**	San Diego
XXIII	1988	**San Francisco**	Cincinnati	**20–16**	South Florida
XXIV	1989	**San Francisco**	Denver	**55–10**	New Orleans
XXV	1990	**N.Y. Giants**	Buffalo	**20–19**	Tampa
XXVI	1991	**Washington**	Buffalo	**37–24**	Minneapolis
XXVII	1992	**Dallas**	Buffalo	**52–17**	Pasadena
XXVIII	1993	**Dallas**	Buffalo	**30–13**	Atlanta
XXIX	1994	**San Francisco**	San Diego	**49–26**	South Florida
XXX	1995	**Dallas**	Pittsburgh	**27–17**	Tempe
XXXI	1996	**Green Bay**	New England	**35–21**	New Orleans
XXXII	1997	**Denver**	Green Bay	**31–24**	San Diego
XXXIII	1998	**Denver**	Atlanta	**34–19**	South Florida
XXXIV	1999	**St. Louis**	Tennessee	**23–16**	Atlanta
XXXV	2000	**Baltimore**	N.Y. Giants	**34–7**	Tampa
XXXVI	2001	**New England**	St. Louis	**20–17**	New Orleans
XXXVII	2002	**Tampa Bay**	Oakland	**48–21**	San Diego
XXXVIII	2003	**New England**	Carolina	**32–29**	Houston
XXXIX	2004	**New England**	Philadelphia	**24–21**	Jacksonville
XL	2005	**Pittsburgh**	Seattle	**21–10**	Detroit
XLI	2006	**Indianapolis**	Chicago	**29–17**	South Florida
XLII	2007	**N.Y. Giants**	New England	**17–14**	Glendale, Ariz.
XLIII	2008	**Pittsburgh**	Arizona	**27–23**	Tampa
XLIV	2009	**New Orleans**	Indianapolis	**31–17**	South Florida

COLLEGE FOOTBALL

WHAT A CATCH!
USC's Ronald Johnson snagged this touchdown pass in the Trojans' game against Oregon State. It was one of many fantastic plays in a great season of college football. Read on for more!

The Alabama Crimson Tide hoists the crystal football as the No. 1 team in the nation!

HOW THE MIGHTY FELL

When the 2009 college football season began, three quarterbacks dominated the headlines. **Sam Bradford** of Oklahoma was the defending Heisman Trophy winner. **Colt McCoy** had led Texas to the 2008 BCS title game. And Florida's **Tim Tebow** (see box) already had two national titles and was aiming for a third.

By the end of the season, none of them was left standing on the field. Just shows that you never know what's going to happen in sports.

The biggest blow came on September 5, when Bradford injured his shoulder in a game against BYU. Oklahoma's title hopes disappeared, even though Bradford tried to come back later that fall. Tebow looked like he might have a shot at title No. 3, but couldn't solve the riddle of the Alabama defense in the Southeastern Conference title game (see page 60). And McCoy's dreams of being the last man standing ended with an early exit from the BCS Championship Game.

In the end, it was Alabama and unheralded QB **Greg McElroy** who carried home the crystal football and the national championship. McElroy, of course, had a lot of help—star running back **Mark Ingram** and a tough D. The Crimson Tide won their eighth national championship while the three star passers could only sit and watch.

Alabama almost didn't reach that game. They could thank noseguard **Terence**

Cody for a crucial field-goal block that clinched a win over Tennessee on October 24. Texas had to hold off Nebraska with a last-play field goal to win the Big 12 and earn a spot in the title game.

The inability of the big three to carry home the trophy just shows how college football is always packed with surprises!

“ We've been up and we've been down. I never would have imagined that we'd have a chance to be in this position. We appreciate every bit of it. ”
— ALABAMA LB
CORY REAMER

FINAL 2009 TOP 10
(From the Associated Press)

1. **Alabama**
2. **Texas**
3. **Florida**
4. **Boise State**
5. **Ohio State**
6. **TCU**
7. **Iowa**
8. **Cincinnati**
9. **Penn State**
10. **Virginia Tech**

Best Collegian Ever?

One of the best things about sports is arguing about stuff like this: Was **Tim Tebow** the best college football player ever? His amazing four seasons at Florida tell a pretty convincing story. He won one Heisman Trophy and was in the top five of the voting for two others. He led his team to two national titles and came within a game of a third. He was the first player to run for 20 TDs and pass for 20 TDs in one season (2007). He ran for more TDs than any QB ever. He's the SEC leader in touchdowns, rushing touchdowns, and total offense. And he's Florida's all-time leader in points scored. Tebow wrapped up his amazing career with a BCS record of 533 yards of total offense in Florida's 51–24 Sugar Bowl win.

Maybe his coach is biased, but here's what **Urban Meyer** thinks about his star QB. "I don't know if there will ever be another one like him—certainly not in my lifetime," Meyer said. "He's the best ambassador I've ever seen of college football."

2009 MAJOR BOWL GAMES

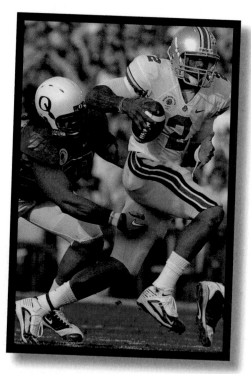

Allstate Sugar Bowl
Florida 51, Cincinnati 24

◀◀◀Rose Bowl
Ohio State 26, Oregon 17

Capital One Bowl
Penn State 19, LSU 17

Tostitos Fiesta Bowl
Boise State 17, TCU 10

FedEx Orange Bowl
Iowa 24, Georgia Tech 14

MORE FOOTBALL TROPHIES

Football Championship Subdivision
Villanova 23, Montana 21▶▶▶

Division II
Northwest Missouri State 30, Grand Valley State 23

Division III
Wisconsin-Whitewater 38, Mount Union 28

The Tide Rolls Over Colt

The 2009 college football championship was basically decided only five plays into the Bowl Championship Series title game. That's when a hit by the Alabama defense knocked Texas QB **Colt McCoy** out of the game. McCoy was the heart and soul of the Longhorns' offense, and with him on the sidelines, their attack sputtered. Alabama took full advantage, sweeping to a 24–6 halftime lead. They never looked back.

After McCoy was injured, freshman **Garrett Gilbert** had to come on. He had thrown only a few passes during the season. Only a year after leading his high school to a Texas state title, Gilbert had all the eyes of Texas on him. He battled, but in the end couldn't rally the Longhorns.

Gilbert did throw two TD passes in the second half. However, he also threw four interceptions, was sacked late in the game, and then fumbled, ending Texas's last chance at a comeback.

For its part, Alabama won the way it had won all season: with a powerful defense and a pounding running game. The D hounded Gilbert all over the field. Heisman Trophy winner **Mark Ingram** (see page 65) rumbled for 116 yards and two scores, while **Trent Richardson** had 109 yards and two more short TDs. The final score of 37–21 looks like a rout, but put McCoy in there and things might have turned out differently.

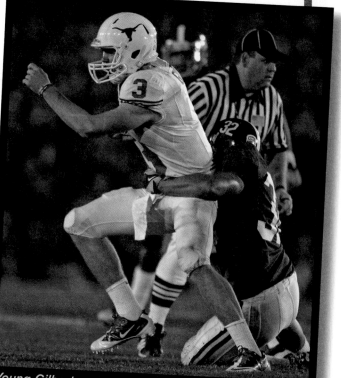

Young Gilbert was swallowed up by 'Bama's D.

CHALK TALK

Championship Game Drama

Big 12 Wow! That's all that can be said about the dramatic Big 12 Championship Game. It took video replay, a long field goal, and a little Longhorn luck to send Texas on to the BCS title game. They beat Nebraska 13–12 on **Hunter Lawrence**'s 46-yard field goal as time ran

out. Texas got one second put back on the clock after **Colt McCoy** threw the ball out of bounds to stop the clock . . . or so he thought. The clock actually ticked to zero, but the officials checked and Texas got its second back. Just enough for a game-winning kick.

◄◄◄**Big East** Down by 21, Cincinnati charged back to defeat Pitt and earn its second straight conference title. A 29-yard touchdown catch by **Armon Binns** with 33 seconds left won it. A missed extra point by Pitt after its final TD proved to be the difference in the 45–44 score.

SEC In what many saw as part one of an NCAA play-off, No. 1 Florida faced No. 2 Alabama in the SEC Championship Game. It was pretty much over by halftime, as 'Bama bounced the Gators 32–13 behind the great running of **Mark Ingram** (see page 65). Alabama didn't let the powerful Florida offense score at all in the second half.

Thought These Guys Were Smart!

New England Patriots coach **Bill Belichick** was not the only man with a clipboard who made a bad call on the field in 2009. With a little more than two minutes left in "The Game," as the annual Harvard-Yale gridiron clash is called, Yale coach **Tom Williams** called for a fake punt. At the time, Yale led 10–7. The fake didn't work, and Harvard got the ball back on its own 40-yard line. They drove down quickly for what proved to be the winning touchdown.

AMAZING UPSETS

One of the great things about college football is the chance for the big upset. The games in which a big power falls to a scrappy underdog are what make fall Saturdays dramatic and exciting. Here are a few memorable upsets from 2009.

WASHINGTON OVER USC ▶▶▶

The Trojans were ranked No. 3 in the country; the Huskies were coming off one of the worst seasons in college football history. Washington proved that history didn't matter and won on a last-play field goal, 16–13.

VIRGINIA OVER UNC

Winless entering their game against ACC rival North Carolina, Virginia tossed out the records . . . and the Tar Heels. A smothering defense led to a surprising 16–3 upset win for the Cavaliers.

PURDUE OVER OSU

Big Ten battles are always tough. No. 7 Ohio State did not expect their game against Purdue to be too hard, however. Purdue had only one win entering the game, while Ohio State expected to be in the hunt for a national title. Five Buckeye turnovers and a great Boilermaker performance later . . . and a 26–18 upset was in the books.

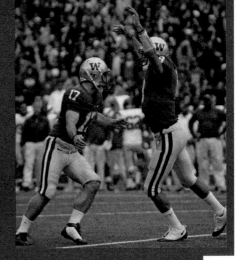

Terrific Toby

Stanford running back **Toby Gerhart** had one of the best seasons of any player in recent years. Many experts thought he could have won the Heisman Trophy that went to **Mark Ingram** of Alabama (see page 65). As it was, Gerhart created a legend with his amazing final season at Stanford. His 28 touchdowns and 1,871 rushing yards led the Bowl Championship Series.

FIVE BIG MOMENTS

Bowden Bows Out

1 Florida State coach **Bobby Bowden** ended one of the most successful runs in college football history. Bowden had led the Seminoles for 34 years. His career total of 389 wins is the second highest of all time, and his record of 33 straight winning seasons was also the most ever. After planting the traditional Seminole spear in the turf before the game, Bowden ended his career by leading FSU to a victory in the Gator Bowl.

Sam's Shoulder

2 During the first game of the 2009 season, the Oklahoma Sooners' hopes for a national title pretty much blinked out. QB **Sam Bradford**, the 2008 Heisman Trophy winner, injured his shoulder in a game against BYU. Though he tried to come back later in the season, Bradford could not play with his usual skill and Oklahoma finished 8–5.

Tragedy in Connecticut

3 The University of Connecticut team had to deal with something unimaginable. In October, defensive back **Jasper Howard** was killed during a street fight. The loss of their teammate stunned the Huskies. But they rallied in his memory and pulled off some upsets. UConn finished the season with a surprising 8–5 record, including a 20–7 bowl-game victory over South Carolina. The Huskies all wore Howard's initials on their uniforms.

Block That Kick ... Twice!

4 Alabama ended up the national champion, but if not for big **Terence Cody**, they might have missed the chance. The massive noseguard (365 pounds) rose up to block not one, but two field-goal tries by Tennessee. The last came on the final play of the game as Alabama held on to win 12–10.

Big House ... Big Game

5 In an exciting September matchup at Michigan Stadium, known as "The Big House," Notre Dame had the ball and the lead, 34–31, with less than three minutes to go in this big rivalry game. However, they chose to throw the ball instead of run and chew up time. Michigan got the ball back with just over two minutes left. They drove down the field and scored a game winner with 11 seconds left!

BY THE NUMBERS

FBS leaders in key stat categories:

44 TOUCHDOWN PASSES
Case KEENUM, Houston ▶▶▶

5,671 PASSING YARDS
Case KEENUM, Houston

1,871 RUSHING YARDS
Toby GERHART, Stanford

155 RECEPTIONS
Freddie BARNES, Bowling Green

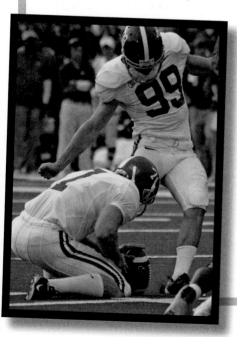

1,781 RECEIVING YARDS
Danario ALEXANDER, Missouri

28 TOUCHDOWNS
Toby GERHART, Stanford

30 FIELD GOALS
◀◀◀ **Leigh TIFFIN**, Alabama

162 TACKLES
Carmen MESSINA, New Mexico

CONFERENCE CHAMPS

ATLANTIC COAST **GEORGIA TECH**

The Ramblin' Wreck won the Coastal Division, while Clemson won the Atlantic. Boston College and Virginia Tech gave those schools fights right down to the wire but ultimately fell short. In an exciting conference championship game, Tech tamed the Tigers, 39–34.

BIG EAST **CINCINNATI**

The Bearcats were one of the biggest surprises of the 2009 season, putting together a perfect 7–0 record in the Big East and a school-record 12–1 overall mark. They dominated the Big East but almost let Pitt slip into a bowl game during a dramatic championship game (see page 60).

BIG TEN **OHIO STATE**

The Buckeyes survived a stunning upset to Purdue to win another Big Ten title. Iowa came on strong, but early-season losses were too much for the Hawkeyes to make up.

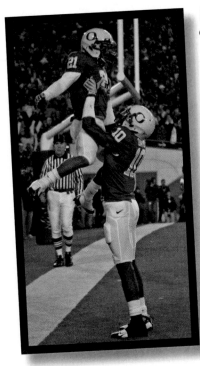

BIG 12 **TEXAS**

On its way to the BCS Championship Game, Texas was a perfect 8–0 in the South Division of the Big 12. In the North Division, Nebraska bowled to a 6–2 record. In a memorable conference championship game, Texas dodged a bullet (see page 60) to win the Big 12 for the third time (and win its 32nd conference title in all).

◄◄◄ PAC-10 **OREGON**

USC's string of seven consecutive conference titles came to an end. The Trojans' upset losses to Washington and Stanford doomed their repeat bid. That left Oregon and Oregon State's in-state "Civil War" rivalry game to decide the conference title. The Ducks quacked last and headed to the Rose Bowl.

SOUTHEASTERN **ALABAMA**

This was a tale of two teams. The tough SEC schedule left only Alabama and Florida undefeated in their divisions. Their matchup in the SEC Championship Game was one of the best games of the season . . . though Florida fans might disagree!

'Bama's Best

Since 1935, when the first Heisman Trophy was given to the top college player in the country, all Alabama players have gone home empty-handed. That surprising "jinx" ended in 2009.

Alabama running back **Mark Ingram** became the first player from the Crimson Tide to take home the trophy. He was also only the second player to win the Heisman and the BCS national championship in the same year (USC QB **Matt Leinart** also doubled up in 2004). Plus, he was the first running back to grab a Heisman and a national title since Pitt's **Tony Dorsett** in 1976.

Ingram whomped opponents, but he was knocked back by the emotion of winning the award. At the award ceremony in New York City, he fought back tears as he thanked his family and teammates for their help.

What's Up in 2010?

With the "big three" QBs moving on to the NFL, look for other big names to come up in 2010. RB **Mark Ingram** will return, so he'll try to match Ohio State's **Archie Griffin** (1974–75) as a two-time Heisman winner. Alabama returns with many other starters, so they'll start out on top and try to stay there. Will 2010 be the year that Boise State finally makes it to the top? They've had two undefeated seasons, and their high-scoring QB **Kellen Moore** (left) returns. Ohio State will make a run, led by star QB **Terrelle Pryor**. Possible surprise teams? A return to glory for Miami, continuing success from Stanford, and, yes, a possible star season from Navy!

WE'RE NO.1

These are the teams that have finished at the top of the Associated Press's final rankings since the poll was first introduced in 1936.

SEASON	TEAM	RECORD	SEASON	TEAM	RECORD
1936	Minnesota	7–1	1973	Notre Dame	11–0
1937	Pittsburgh	9–0–1	1974	Oklahoma	11–0
1938	Texas Christian	11–0	1975	Oklahoma	11–1
1939	Texas A&M	11–0	1976	Pittsburgh	12–0
1940	Minnesota	8–0	1977	Notre Dame	11–1
1941	Minnesota	8–0	1978	Alabama	11–1
1942	Ohio State	9–1	1979	Alabama	12–0
1943	Notre Dame	9–1	1980	Georgia	12–0
1944	Army	9–0	1981	Clemson	12–0
1945	Army	9–0	1982	Penn State	11–1
1946	Notre Dame	8–0–1	1983	Miami	11–1
1947	Notre Dame	9–0	1984	Brigham Young	13–0
1948	Michigan	9–0	1985	Oklahoma	11–1
1949	Notre Dame	10–0	1986	Penn State	12–0
1950	Oklahoma	10–1	1987	Miami	12–0
1951	Tennessee	10–1	1988	Notre Dame	12–0
1952	Michigan State	9–0	1989	Miami	11–1
1953	Maryland	10–1	1990	Colorado	11–1–1
1954	Ohio State	10–0	1991	Miami	12–0
1955	Oklahoma	11–0	1992	Alabama	13–0
1956	Oklahoma	10–0	1993	Florida State	12–1
1957	Auburn	10–0	1994	Nebraska	13–0
1958	LSU	11–0	1995	Nebraska	12–0
1959	Syracuse	11–0	1996	Florida	12–1
1960	Minnesota	8–2	1997	Michigan	12–0
1961	Alabama	11–0	1998	Tennessee	13–0
1962	USC	11–0	1999	Florida State	12–0
1963	Texas	11–0	2000	Oklahoma	13–0
1964	Alabama	10–1	2001	Miami	12–0
1965	Alabama	9–1–1	2002	Ohio State	14–0
1966	Notre Dame	9–0–1	2003	USC	12–1
1967	USC	10–1	2004	USC	13–0
1968	Ohio State	10–0	2005	Texas	13–0
1969	Texas	11–0	2006	Florida	13–1
1970	Nebraska	11–0–1	2007	LSU	10–2
1971	Nebraska	13–0	2008	Florida	13–1
1972	USC	12–0	2009	Alabama	14–0

BOWL CHAMPIONSHIP SERIES
NATIONAL CHAMPIONSHIP GAMES

College football (at its highest level) is one of the few sports that doesn't have an on-field play-off to determine its champion. In the 1998 season, the NCAA introduced the Bowl Championship Series (BCS), which matches the top two teams in the title game according to a complicated formula that takes into account records, polls, and computer rankings. At the end of the regular season, the teams ranked No. 1 and No. 2 meet in a championship game, usually during the first week of January after all the major bowl games have been played. Here are the results of all the BCS title games.

SEASON	SCORE	SITE
1998	**Tennessee 23, Florida State 16**	TEMPE, AZ
1999	**Florida State 46, Virginia Tech 29**	NEW ORLEANS, LA
2000	**Oklahoma 13, Florida State 2**	MIAMI, FL
2001	**Miami 37, Nebraska 14**	PASADENA, CA
2002	**Ohio State 31, Miami 24**	TEMPE, AZ
2003	**LSU 21, Oklahoma 14**	NEW ORLEANS, LA
2004	**USC 55, Oklahoma 19**	MIAMI, FL
2005	**Texas 41, USC 38**	PASADENA, CA
2006	**Florida 41, Ohio State 14**	GLENDALE, AZ
2007	**LSU 38, Ohio State 24**	NEW ORLEANS, LA
2008	**Florida 24, Oklahoma 14**	MIAMI, FL
2009	**Alabama 37, Texas 21**	PASADENA, CA

NEARLY A MIRACLE
With time running out and the whole nation watching, Butler's Gordon Hayward launched this final shot in the 2010 NCAA championship game. From behind half-court, it almost went in! As the ball clanged off the rim, Duke became the champion, and Butler remained a wonderful, if unfinished, Cinderella story. Its marvelous, unexpected run to the title game capped off a terrific college hoops season.

COLLEGE BASKETBALL

HOOP DREAMS

Gordon Hayward's last-second half-court heave sailed through the air long enough for fans to dream of the possibilities. When the Butler forward lofted the potential game-winning shot in the NCAA title game versus mighty Duke, he was acting out the fantasy of every boy and girl who had ever picked up a basketball.

Hayward's heave barely missed. Duke won its fourth NCAA championship under coach **Mike Krzyzewski**. Still, March Madness lived up to its name in 2010. Following a regular season in which no team emerged as dominant, the tournament itself became the star attraction.

Four different schools were ranked No. 1 at some stage of the year: Kansas, Texas, Kentucky, and Syracuse. None of them got as far as the Final Four. In early January, Kansas found itself trailing at home with less than a minute to play against Cornell of the Ivy League. Kansas, owners of the nation's longest home winning streak (50 games), barely won.

And, as the season wore on, Cornell proved to be a worthy adversary. The Big Red advanced to the Sweet Sixteen in the NCAAs before losing to Kentucky.

The Wildcats themselves balanced invincibility with inexperience. Kentucky started four freshmen and won its first 19 games. Led by dazzling point guard **John Wall**, they advanced to the Elite Eight before losing to

Coach K and his Blue Devils celebrate their fourth NCAA championship.

West Virginia. After the season, all four freshmen declared themselves eligible for the NBA Draft. They were following the NCAA's rule of "one and done"—that is, players have to play at least one NCAA season before jumping to the NBA. Other college superstars headed early to the NBA this fall include **Xavier Henry** of Kansas and **Derrick Favors** of Georgia Tech.

Evan Turner turned around a potentially lost season at Ohio State. In early December, the Buckeye guard fractured two bones in his back when he fell following a dunk. Turner was supposed to be out for two months. He was back in half that time and won all the major Player of the Year hardware handed out at season's end (see box on page 75).

When March Madness arrived, surprise teams Cornell and St. Mary's both survived the opening weekend with the same recipe:

John Wall was "one"derful . . . and done.

MEN'S FINAL TOP 10

Final ESPN/*USA Today* Coaches' Poll

1. Duke
2. Butler
3. West Virginia
4. Michigan State
5. Kentucky
6. Kansas
7. Kansas State
8. Syracuse
9. Tennessee
10. Baylor

seven-foot centers and perimeter players with stunning accuracy from beyond the arc.

No team, however, turned the world upside down quite like Northern Iowa. The Panthers shocked No. 1 overall seed Kansas in the second round. Leading by just a point with 34 seconds to play, Northern Iowa guard **Ali Farokhmanesh** buried a three-pointer. Such brazen confidence, from a six-foot guard who was not even recruited out of high school, typified the "One Shining Moment" ideal of the tournament.

By the time Hayward launched his and Butler's shot at immortality two weeks later . . . well, it would be greedy to expect another such thrill. The glass sneaker just didn't fit that particular Cinderella.

MARCH MADNESS!

Duke's Nolan Smith sails to the hoop!

The biggest news as the 2010 NCAA men's basketball championship began was not who was in . . . but who was out! Indiana, North Carolina, and UCLA, who have each won at least five NCAA championships, did not hear their names called on Selection Sunday. Arizona, who had been invited to March Madness for 25 straight years, also stayed home. Once play began, injuries were an unfortunate part of this tournament. Several key players were hurt, helping end their team's hopes. Purdue lost **Robbie Hummel**, Michigan State suffered the loss of **Kalin Lucas**, and Syracuse couldn't play its best without **Arinze Onuaku**. In one of the national semifinals, **Da'Sean Butler** of West Virginia was hurt. As he lay on the floor in pain, his coach, **Bob Huggins**, gave the sports world one of its most emotional moments of the year. Huggins kneeled over Butler, comforting his star as the nation watched.

But even with big names missing and key players falling, play went on, and it turned out to be one of the most entertaining tournaments in recent years. Cinderella teams always get a lot of attention at the tournament, and 2010 was no exception. The St. Mary's team made the Sweet Sixteen, impressing fans with

Tough Picks!
Just how difficult is it to fill out an NCAA tournament bracket correctly? In a season with no truly dominant teams, 4.78 million brackets were filled out on ESPN.com. After the opening weekend of play, which consisted of 48 games in the first two rounds, not one of those nearly 5 million brackets remained perfect.

UP NEXT

2011 Final Four
Reliant Stadium, Houston, Texas

The big news is that the tournament expands to 68 teams, from 65 in 2010. That means that 3 more teams have a shot at becoming the new Butler!

State on the way to the Final Four. In the national semifinals, they schooled Michigan State and earned the first championship game spot by a mid-major since 2006.

In the final game against mighty Duke, Butler continued to battle, surprising many fans by keeping the game close throughout. But Duke pulled ahead late in the game, and a furious Butler rally fell short. After Duke took a final 61–59 lead on a free throw by **Brian Zoubek**, **Gordon Hayward** of Butler just barely missed a half-court dream shot. Even with the loss, Butler earned enormous respect. Meanwhile, Duke gained its fourth national title and Coach K tied for the second-most titles ever by a coach.

its outside shooting and hard work. Ivy champion Cornell was another surprise in the Sweet Sixteen, with wins over Temple and Wisconsin.

No player in the NCAA tournament charmed fans—and the media—quite like seven-footer **Omar Samhan** of St. Mary's. Samhan, who lost sixty pounds between his freshman and senior years, led the Gaels to the Sweet Sixteen. He scored 29 points against No. 7 seed Richmond and then 32 points versus No. 2 seed Villanova. "I've had tons of e-mails saying I can't believe you won, you messed up my bracket," said Samhan. "And that's from my mom."

The biggest upset was Northern Iowa over Kansas, picked by many to win the tournament. Kansas kept trying to rally to win, but Northern Iowa's pinpoint outside shooting kept the Jayhawks back. The capper was the three-point shot that **Ali Farokhmanesh** nailed with 34 seconds left. Unguarded and open, he could have dribbled to use up time, but he decided to slam the door on Kansas with a huge three.

Butler, of course, was the biggest story of the tournament. The Bulldogs knocked off a series of big-name basketball powers, gaining fans as they went. Down went UCLA, Ohio State, Syracuse, and Kansas

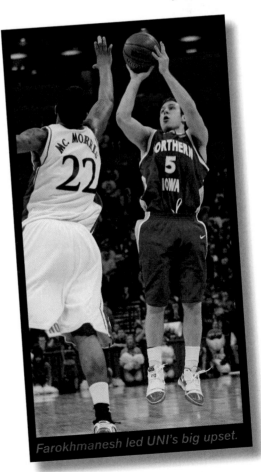

Farokhmanesh led UNI's big upset.

Block Party ▶▶▶

Hassan Whiteside (21) did not play in the NCAA tournament, and he almost never appeared on national TV. However, Marshall's seven-foot freshman led the nation in blocked shots with 182. Whiteside grew nearly a foot after eighth grade and is still growing. His 182 blocks are the most in one college season since 1986, when future NBA Hall of Famer **David Robinson** set the record with 207 for Navy.

Coaching Legend

Herb Magee won his 903rd college game, all at Division II Philadelphia University (formerly known as Philadelphia Textile) to pass legendary

coach **Bob Knight**. Magee, in his 43rd season coaching his alma mater, has more victories than any coach in college basketball history. Magee ended the 2010 season with 907 wins.

◀◀◀Long Fall for Longhorns

No school fell harder, or faster, than Texas. On January 18 the Longhorns were 17–0 and ranked No. 1 in the country when they visited hard-nosed Kansas State. The Longhorns lost that night, 71–62, to launch a second-half swoon. They lost 8 of their final 14 games. Then, in the first round of the NCAAs, the Longhorns blew an eight-point lead—in overtime!—against Wake Forest to end their disappointing season with an 81–80 defeat.

Big Shot in the Big Ten

For an Ohio State team that was nearly guaranteed a top seed in the NCAA tourney, a first-round game in the Big Ten tournament may not have meant much. But then the Buckeyes found themselves trailing rival Michigan, 68–66, with 2.2 seconds to go. **Evan Turner**, the consensus National Player of the Year, took an inbounds pass, dribbled twice, and launched a 37-footer as time expired. *Swish!* The Buckeyes went on to win the Big Ten tourney before losing to Tennessee in the Sweet Sixteen.

Long-Distance

Small-conference teams rarely travel outside their schools' time zones. It's too expensive. So no one can quite explain why Marist, which is located in Albany, N.Y., flew cross-country (2,800 miles) to play UC Irvine on a Saturday in February. The visiting Red Foxes, who entered the game with a 1–25 record, lost by one point, 66–65. Either way, it was going to be a long flight home.

BIG-TIME BUCKEYE

Before the season, many experts picked **Evan Turner** to be one of the top players in the nation. That prediction was in doubt one December evening as Turner lay on the wooden floor in obvious pain. Falling after a dunk, he had broken two bones in his lower back. It looked like his season was over, and with it any chance of top-player honors.

But Turner was not going to take this lying down . . . literally. He worked hard to get back to the court, and surprised his doctors and everyone else by playing again just three weeks later, missing only six games. He led Ohio State to the Big Ten championship, winning one game with a huge, last-second shot. Though he and the Buckeyes fell to Tennessee in the NCAA tournament, Turner's skills and guts were obvious to all. He won the Naismith and Wooden Awards as the nation's top player. Look for him to continue his great career in the NBA in 2010.

RECORD RUN

After another perfect season, UConn did a dance!

stars in the women's game. Stanford was forging an almost equally dominant record, knocking off team after team by big margins. In fact, Stanford's only loss before it met UConn in the final . . . was to UConn in November.

In Texas, Baylor freshman **Brittney Griner** was putting her name in the record books for blocking shots. The 6'8" forward ended up with a total of 223 blocks on the season, the most ever by a woman at any level in college hoops history. She also set a record by blocking 40 shots in the NCAA tournament! She also averaged 16.8 points per game. Look for her to keep making a big mark on women's basketball in 2010.

In the NCAA tournament, no team really challenged UConn until the final game. Stanford came into the game ranked second in the country. For the first half of the game, the Cardinal didn't pay any attention to UConn's streak, rushing out to a stunning 18–9 lead. In fact, after the first half, UConn had

Wow. That's all you can say about what the University of Connecticut women's team has done in the past two seasons.

Wow.

In those two years, no team has beaten the Huskies. UConn has won 78 straight games, beating its own record by 7. Even more amazing, the Huskies won each of those games (except the last one) by at least 10 points. The next record the team, led by coach **Geno Auriemma**, is eyeing is the 88-game record of the UCLA men's team (1971–1974). With a returning core of players and amazing recruits, it looks like that's another record that is ready to be broken.

For the 2009–10 season, UConn was the dominant story, but there were other

Brittney Griner

HUSKIES HEROINE

Tina Charles powers to the hoop!

Connecticut has had a ton of awesome players as it mowed down opponents for two seasons, winning back-to-back national titles. It's no surprise, then, that one of them is the best in the nation. For the second year in a row, a UConn athlete was named the National Player of the Year. For 2010, it was forward **Tina Charles**.

Charles proved to be a powerful inside force, averaging 18.4 points, most from close range, while pulling down an awesome 9.5 rebounds per game. She finished ahead of teammate and 2009 Player of the Year **Maya Moore** in the voting for the award.

The good news for Connecticut's next opponents is that next season, Charles will be playing for the Connecticut Sun in the WNBA. She was chosen number one overall in that league's draft in April . . . and she won't even have to move out of the Nutmeg State!

managed to score only 12 points and was trailing by 8. That total was the fewest points ever by a UConn team in a first half.

However, the experienced Huskies, led by Player of the Year **Tina Charles** (see box) and superstar **Maya Moore**, roared back. They outscored Stanford, 17–2, to start the second half. Charles dominated on the boards, while Moore buried a three-point shot that finally gave her team the lead. Moore ended up with 23 points and was named the tournament's most outstanding player. Stanford seemed to wilt a bit after that, and Connecticut rambled to its seventh title, 53–47. The Huskies were the first women's team ever to win back-to-back titles after undefeated seasons.

As they cut down the nets, all you could think was . . . wow.

WOMEN'S FINAL TOP 10

1. Connecticut
2. Stanford
3. Oklahoma
4. Baylor
5. Xavier
6. Duke
7. Nebraska
8. Tennessee
9. Kentucky (TIE)
   Florida State (TIE)

NCAA CHAMPS

MEN'S DIVISION I

North Carolina's players celebrate after winning the 2009 title.

2010 **Duke**	2001 **Duke**
2009 **North Carolina**	2000 **Michigan State**
2008 **Kansas**	1999 **Connecticut**
2007 **Florida**	1998 **Kentucky**
2006 **Florida**	1997 **Arizona**
2005 **North Carolina**	1996 **Kentucky**
2004 **Connecticut**	1995 **UCLA**
2003 **Syracuse**	1994 **Arkansas**
2002 **Maryland**	1993 **North Carolina**

1992 **Duke**
1991 **Duke**
1990 **UNLV**
1989 **Michigan**
1988 **Kansas**
1987 **Indiana**
1986 **Louisville**
1985 **Villanova**
1984 **Georgetown**
1983 **NC State**
1982 **North Carolina**
1981 **Indiana**
1980 **Louisville**
1979 **Michigan State**
1978 **Kentucky**
1977 **Marquette**
1976 **Indiana**
1975 **UCLA**
1974 **NC State**
1973 **UCLA**

1972 **UCLA**	1949 **Kentucky**	1943 **Wyoming**
1971 **UCLA**	1948 **Kentucky**	1942 **Stanford**
1970 **UCLA**	1947 **Holy Cross**	1941 **Wisconsin**
1969 **UCLA**	1946 **Oklahoma A&M**	1940 **Indiana**
1968 **UCLA**	1945 **Oklahoma A&M**	1939 **Oregon**
1967 **UCLA**	1944 **Utah**	
1966 **Texas Western**		
1965 **UCLA**		

WOMEN'S DIVISION I

1964 **UCLA**	2010 **Connecticut**	1995 **Connecticut**
1963 **Loyola (Illinois)**	2009 **Connecticut**	1994 **North Carolina**
1962 **Cincinnati**	2008 **Tennessee**	1993 **Texas Tech**
1961 **Cincinnati**	2007 **Tennessee**	1992 **Stanford**
1960 **Ohio State**	2006 **Maryland**	1991 **Tennessee**
1959 **California**	2005 **Baylor**	1990 **Stanford**
1958 **Kentucky**	2004 **Connecticut**	1989 **Tennessee**
1957 **North Carolina**	2003 **Connecticut**	1988 **Louisiana Tech**
1956 **San Francisco**	2002 **Connecticut**	1987 **Tennessee**
1955 **San Francisco**	2001 **Notre Dame**	1986 **Texas**
1954 **La Salle**	2000 **Connecticut**	1985 **Old Dominion**
1953 **Indiana**	1999 **Purdue**	1984 **USC**
1952 **Kansas**	1998 **Tennessee**	1983 **USC**
1951 **Kentucky**	1997 **Tennessee**	1982 **Louisiana Tech**
1950 **City Coll. of N.Y.**	1996 **Tennessee**	

TO THE RACK!
Kobe Bryant of the Los Angeles Lakers (right) levitates above Rasheed Wallace of the Boston Celtics during the NBA Finals. The Lakers won their 16th NBA title by defeating their longtime archrivals in seven exciting games. Bryant was named the MVP of the Finals.

NBA

SWEET SIXTEEN!

Hey, Lakers! Make room on the trophy shelf for No. 16!

Game 7 of the NBA Finals. Lakers. Celtics. The league's two most famous teams battling, with the season and history on the line, in front of the largest NBA TV audience in 12 years. This time the Los Angeles Lakers prevailed, beating the Boston Celtics, 83–79, for their 16th league championship and 2nd in a row.

"We did it with perseverance," said Lakers coach **Phil Jackson**, who won his 11th overall title, the most ever by a coach in a major American sport.

Speaking of records, the Lakers are now just one crown shy of the Celtics' league-record 17 titles. **Kobe Bryant**, who was named the Finals MVP, averaged 28.6 points over the seven games and snagged 15 rebounds in Game 7. This was also Bryant's

fifth championship—just one shy of **Michael Jordan**. The Celtics and the Lakers have met in the Finals 12 times. The first was way back in 1962. The most recent before this latest showdown came in 2008, when the Celtics won.

Bryant and the Lakers stopped the Celtics from an epic run to the title. Boston had limped to the end of the 2009–10 regular season, going 3–7 in its last 10 games. But, led by veterans **Kevin Garnett**, **Ray Allen**, and **Paul Pierce**, they came alive in the play-offs.

In the Eastern Conference Semifinals, they defeated the Cleveland Cavaliers, 4–2. The Cavs had finished with a league-best 61 wins. **LeBron James** was crowned league MVP for the second season in a row after averaging 29.7 points and a career-high 8.6 assists. The addition of center Shaquille O'Neal in the off-season was intended to give Cleveland a one-two punch. But the Celtics put the brakes on the Cavs. It was a tough end to what turned out to be James's last year in Cleveland (see box).

In the Eastern Conference Finals, the Celtics defeated the Orlando Magic, 4–2, despite the dynamite play of **Dwight Howard**. In his sixth NBA season, the super center led the league in rebounds (13.2) and blocks (2.78).

Forward **Kevin Durant** and the Oklahoma City Thunder stormed into the

They're Back!

The biggest news in the NBA (other than the Lakers' victory) was where **LeBron James** landed. After his contract in Cleveland was up, James kept fans on the edge of their seats before announcing that he would play the 2010-11 season in Miami. In Los Angeles, Lakers fans were relieved when coach **Phil Jackson**, who has won 11 NBA titles, said that he would return for one final season.

spotlight in 2009–10. Although they lost in the first round of the play-offs to the Lakers (4–2), the Thunder finished 50–32, more than doubling their win total from the previous season. (The 2008–09 season was their first in Oklahoma City. They relocated from Seattle as the SuperSonics in 2008). Durant led the young team and the league in scoring (30.1 points per game).

See ya, Cleveland . . . I'm taking my ball and going to play with my friends in Miami!

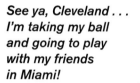

2009-10 FINAL STANDINGS

EASTERN CONFERENCE

ATLANTIC DIVISION	W	L
Boston	50	32
Toronto	40	42
New York	29	53
Philadelphia	27	55
New Jersey	12	70

CENTRAL DIVISION	W	L
Cleveland	61	21
Milwaukee	46	36
Chicago	41	41
Indiana	32	50
Detroit	27	55

SOUTHEAST DIVISION	W	L
Orlando	59	23
Atlanta	53	29
Miami	47	35
Charlotte	44	38
Washington	26	56

WESTERN CONFERENCE

NORTHWEST DIVISION	W	L
Denver	53	29
Utah	53	29
Portland	50	32
Oklahoma City	50	32
Minnesota	15	67

PACIFIC DIVISION	W	L
L.A. Lakers	57	25
Phoenix	54	28
L.A. Clippers	29	53
Golden State	26	56
Sacramento	25	57

SOUTHWEST DIVISION	W	L
Dallas	55	27
San Antonio	50	32
Houston	42	40
Memphis	40	42
New Orleans	37	45

THE PLAY-OFFS

The Lakers' return to the NBA Finals was not a guarantee. Seven other teams in the Western Conference finished with 50 or more wins. And although L.A. finished with 57 wins—tops in the Western Conference—that was still eight wins less than it had in the previous season.

And then the play-offs began, and all doubt was cast aside. The Lakers beat the Oklahoma City Thunder, 4–2, in the first round, silenced the Jazz in round two, 4–0, and then set down the Suns in six games.

The Finals against the Celtics was a series for the record books. Using a swarming defense in the first game, the Lakers shut down Boston 102–89. But the Celtics tied the series in Game 2 behind the shooting of **Ray Allen**. Allen finished with a game-high 32 points, 27 of which came in the first half. He also set an NBA Finals record for most three-pointers in a game by going 8-for-11 from behind the arc. Game 3 went to the Lakers, but the Celtics held on for victories in Games 4 and 5. But when the Lakers returned to their home court, they were able to surge back for a win. L.A. won the final game, 83–79, outscoring their rival, 30–22, in the final period. In their 12 previous Finals meetings, the Lakers and Celtics had gone to seven games four times . . . but the Lakers had never won a Game 7!

Leading up to their Finals appearance, the Celtics looked as impressive as the Lakers on their journey. They lost just five games in the first three rounds. Their best series came against the Cleveland Cavaliers in the Eastern Conference Semifinals. The Cavs had 11 more wins than Boston in the regular season. They also had the league's best player and MVP **LeBron James**. But Boston dominated the last two games to take the series, 4–2. Boston's rising star,

"Now I've got just one more than Shaq. You can take that to the bank!"

— KOBE BRYANT

Rajon Rondo led the Celtics past Cleveland.

PLAY-OFF RESULTS
(Games won in parentheses)

FIRST ROUND

EASTERN CONFERENCE

Cleveland OVER Chicago (4-1)

Orlando OVER Charlotte (4-0)

Atlanta OVER Milwaukee (4-3)

Boston OVER Miami (4-1)

WESTERN CONFERENCE

L.A. Lakers OVER Oklahoma City (4-2)

Dallas OVER San Antonio (4-2)

Phoenix OVER Portland (4-2)

Utah OVER Denver (4-2)

CONFERENCE SEMIFINALS

EASTERN CONFERENCE

Boston OVER Cleveland (4-2)

Orlando OVER Atlanta (4-0)

WESTERN CONFERENCE

Phoenix OVER San Antonio (4-0)

L.A. Lakers OVER Utah (4-0)

CONFERENCE FINALS

EASTERN CONFERENCE

Boston OVER Orlando (4-2)

WESTERN CONFERENCE

L.A. Lakers OVER Phoenix (4-2)

NBA FINALS

L.A. Lakers OVER Boston (4-3)

Josh Smith helped Atlanta beat Milwaukee.

point guard **Rajon Rondo**, dropped 21 points and dished 12 assists in the final game, while 15-year veteran **Kevin Garnett** added 22 points and grabbed 12 boards.

The only series in the play-offs, besides the Finals, to go to the full seven games came in the first round between the Milwaukee Bucks and the Atlanta Hawks. The Hawks, led by flashy point guard **Joe Johnson**, prevailed, winning Game 7 95–74. But the first-round effort simply wore out the Hawks, and they were swept in the next round by the Magic, 4–0.

BEST OF THE BEST

D-MONSTER

LeBron James may be the King, but **Dwight Howard** of the Orlando Magic is the Wizard. The Defensive Wizard, that is. Howard was named to the All-NBA team for the third straight time. He also became the first player to lead the league in rebounds and blocks in two straight seasons, averaging 13.2 rebounds and 2.78 blocks. Howard led the league with 64 double-doubles (reaching double digits in two stat categories), including three games of at least 20 points and 20 rebounds.

2009-2010 NBA AWARD WINNERS

MOST VALUABLE PLAYER	**LeBron JAMES,** Cleveland
DEFENSIVE PLAYER OF THE YEAR	**Dwight HOWARD,** Orlando
ROOKIE OF THE YEAR	**Tyreke EVANS,** Sacramento
CITIZENSHIP AWARD	**Samuel DALEMBERT,** Philadelphia
SPORTSMANSHIP AWARD	**Grant HILL,** Phoenix
SIXTH MAN AWARD	**Jamal CRAWFORD,** Atlanta
MOST IMPROVED PLAYER	**Aaron BROOKS,** Houston
COACH OF THE YEAR	**Scott BROOKS,** Oklahoma City

All-NBA

LeBron James and **Dwight Howard** were both unanimous choices for All-NBA. **Kevin Durant** made his first All-NBA team. He was the youngest player (21 years, 197 days) to lead the league in scoring (30.1 ppg).

FIRST TEAM
LeBron James, F, CLEVELAND
Kevin Durant, F, OKLAHOMA CITY
Dwight Howard, C, ORLANDO
Kobe Bryant, G, L.A. LAKERS
Dwyane Wade, G, MIAMI

SECOND TEAM
Carmelo Anthony, F, DENVER
Dirk Nowitzki, F, DALLAS
Amáre Stoudemire, C, PHOENIX
Steve Nash, G, PHOENIX
Deron Williams, G, UTAH

THIRD TEAM
Tim Duncan, F, SAN ANTONIO
Pau Gasol, F, L.A. LAKERS
Andrew Bogut, C, MILWAUKEE
Joe Johnson, G, ATLANTA
Brandon Roy, G, PORTLAND

THE LEADERS

The top NBA performers in some key statistical categories for 2009–10:

CATEGORY	PLAYER, TEAM	MARK
SCORING	Kevin DURANT, OKLAHOMA CITY	30.1
REBOUNDS	Dwight HOWARD, Orlando	13.8
ASSISTS	Steve NASH, PHOENIX	11.0
STEALS	Rajon RONDO, BOSTON	2.33
BLOCKS	Dwight HOWARD, ORLANDO	2.78
FIELD-GOAL PCT.	Dwight HOWARD, ORLANDO	.612
3-POINT FG PCT.	Kyle KORVER, UTAH	.536
FREE-THROW PCT.	Steve NASH, PHOENIX	.938

MERCURY RISING

The Phoenix Mercury won their second WNBA title in the past three years. They defeated the Indiana Fever in five games. (The defending champs, the Detroit Shock, fell to the Fever in the Eastern Conference finals.)

How did Phoenix win it all? Two words: **Diana Taurasi**. The league's MVP is an aggressive 6-foot guard and forward who was tops in the league in scoring for the third time in four seasons (20.4 points per game) since joining the WNBA after her championship career at the University of Connecticut. Tough Taurasi led Phoenix's triple-threat offense, joined by guard **Cappie Pondexter**, who finished third in the league in assists per game (5.0), and forward **Penny Taylor**, who averaged 10.9 points per game.

While Phoenix was making history of one kind, the Houston Comets were making history of another: The Comets, who won the first four WNBA league titles in a row (1997–2000) folded in December 2008. This was the league's first season without them.

Diana Taurasi carried Phoenix to the top.

2010 WNBA PLAYERS TO WATCH

⊙ Guard Cappie Pondexter of the Phoenix Mercury joined the New York Liberty in the off-season. A graduate of nearby Rutgers University, she could help the Liberty make a title run.

⊙ Former track and field star Marion Jones, coming back from her steroid troubles, made her WNBA debut with the Tulsa Shock.

⊙ Forward Candace Parker of the Los Angeles Sparks, who missed part of the 2009 season while having a baby, is the new face of the Sparks' franchise. She can score, rebound, and play defense—inside and outside the paint.

Final 2009 Standings

EASTERN CONFERENCE			WESTERN CONFERENCE		
	W	L		W	L
Indiana	22	12	Phoenix	23	11
Atlanta	18	16	Seattle	20	14
Detroit	18	16	Los Angeles	18	16
Washington	16	18	San Antonio	15	19
Chicago	16	18	Minnesota	14	20
Connecticut	16	18	Sacramento	12	22
New York	13	21			

Indiana defensive star Tamika Catchings blocks another shot.

The league also said good-bye to center **Lisa Leslie** of the Los Angeles Sparks. Leslie, who earned three WNBA MVP Awards and two Finals MVP Awards, retired after the season. She had been part of the league since it started in 1997.

Angel McCoughtry, the first pick of the 2009 WNBA Draft, proved to be a dream come true for the Atlanta Dream. The 6'1" forward from Louisville was named the Rookie of the Year after averaging 12.8 points per game. More importantly, she helped Atlanta improve its record from 4–30 in 2008 to 18–16 in 2009.

Veteran forward **Tamika Catchings** of the Indiana Fever won her third Defensive Player of the Year Award. She led the league in steals (2.91) for a record fifth time.

The 2009 season was also the last time the Shock played in Detroit. They moved southwest to Tulsa, Oklahoma, in October 2009.

Lisa Leslie was the WNBA's best all-time player.

STAT STUFF

NBA CHAMPIONS

Center Bill Russell and coach Red Auerbach after a Celtics title.

2001–02 **L.A. Lakers**		1986–87 **L.A. Lakers**
2000–01 **L.A. Lakers**		1985–86 **Boston**
1999–00 **L.A. Lakers**		1984–85 **L.A. Lakers**
1998–99 **San Antonio**		1983–84 **Boston**
1997–98 **Chicago**		1982–83 **Philadelphia**
1996–97 **Chicago**		1981–82 **L.A. Lakers**
1995–96 **Chicago**		1980–81 **Boston**
2009–10 **L.A. Lakers**	1994–95 **Houston**	1979–80 **L.A. Lakers**
2008–09 **L.A. Lakers**	1993–94 **Houston**	1978–79 **Seattle**
2007–08 **Boston**	1992–93 **Chicago**	1977–78 **Washington**
2006–07 **San Antonio**	1991–92 **Chicago**	1976–77 **Portland**
2005–06 **Miami**	1990–91 **Chicago**	1975–76 **Boston**
2004–05 **San Antonio**	1989–90 **Detroit**	1974–75 **Golden State**
2003–04 **Detroit**	1988–89 **Detroit**	1973–74 **Boston**
2002–03 **San Antonio**	1987–88 **L.A. Lakers**	1972–73 **New York**

1971–72 **L.A. Lakers**	1953–54 **Minneapolis**	1949–50 **Minneapolis**
1970–71 **Milwaukee**	1952–53 **Minneapolis**	1948–49 **Minneapolis**
1969–70 **New York**	1951–52 **Minneapolis**	1947–48 **Baltimore**
1968–69 **Boston**	1950–51 **Rochester**	1946–47 **Philadelphia**
1967–68 **Boston**		
1966–67 **Philadelphia**		

WNBA CHAMPIONS

1965–66 **Boston**	
1964–65 **Boston**	
1963–64 **Boston**	
1962–63 **Boston**	
1961–62 **Boston**	
1960–61 **Boston**	
1959–60 **Boston**	
1958–59 **Boston**	
1957–58 **St. Louis**	
1956–57 **Boston**	
1955–56 **Philadelphia**	
1954–55 **Syracuse**	

2009 **Phoenix**	2002 **Los Angeles**
2008 **Detroit**	2001 **Los Angeles**
2007 **Phoenix**	2000 **Houston**
2006 **Detroit**	1999 **Houston**
2005 **Sacramento**	1998 **Houston**
2004 **Seattle**	1997 **Houston**
2003 **Detroit**	

Houston won the first of its four straight titles in 1997.

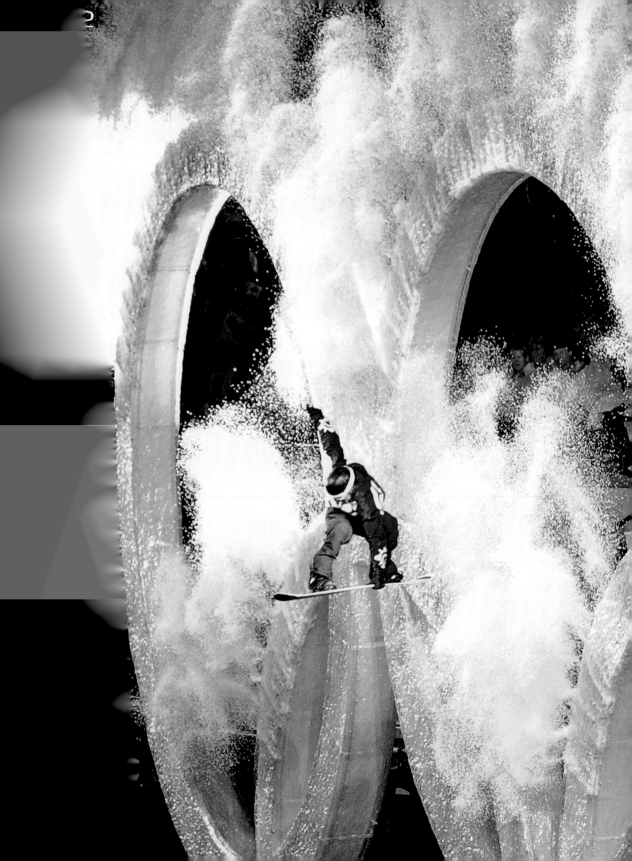

WHAT AN OPENING!

Canadian snowboarder Johnny Lyall got the 2010 Winter Games off to a flying start. He swooped down a ramp and flew right through giant Olympic rings as fireworks and confetti exploded around him! The Winter Olympics in Vancouver, Canada, were a huge success for the U.S. and Canadian teams.

2010 WINTER OLYMPICS

LET IT SNOW....PLEASE!

That's what organizers of the 2010 Winter Olympic Games at Vancouver, Canada, were saying as the February dates of the Games approached. The hills that would be home to skiing events were not packed with snow. However, with a little teamwork, some giant trucks full of manmade snow, and—finally—Mother Nature, the Games were held in a winter wonderland.

The host nation put on a great show, but the biggest story of the Games was the dominant performance of the American Olympians. With 37 total medals (see chart), they set an all-time record for a nation at the Winter Games. U.S. athletes succeeded in sports that have long been American strongholds, such as speed skating. However, they also triumphed in other sports—bobsled and Nordic combined, for example—that they don't

Korean skater Kim Yu-Na set a new record and won gold.

usually do well in. Downhill champ **Lindsey Vonn** was the first big star of the Games, capturing her gold medal in a weather-delayed event that kicked off the two-week snowstravaganza. **Bode Miller** later came through in the combined event, helping U.S. Alpine skiers to their best Olympics ever (see page 96). They were just two of the many U.S. stars who emerged from the snow and ice to find a place in Olympian history.

For its part, Canada led the way with the most gold medals: 14, also a record for a nation at a single Games. Two previous Olympics—Montreal in 1976 and Calgary in 1988—had been held in the Great White North without the home team winning any golds. So when moguls maven **Alexander Bilodeau** won on the first day, it set off a huge celebration.

At every Olympics, figure skating is always a big event. It was no different in Vancouver. The men's program was capped by

TRAGEDY AT THE GAMES

Sadly, the Olympic Games started with a tragedy. In a practice run before his event, luger **Nodar Kumaritashvili** was killed when his sled flew off the track. He hit a steel pole. The entire Olympic community mourned, and honored Kumaritashvili during the Opening and Closing Ceremonies. It was a terrible accident, but one that didn't stop others from continuing to pursue their Olympic dreams, just as Kumaritashvili had been doing.

2010 Winter Olympics Medals

COUNTRY	GOLD	SILVER	BRONZE	TOTAL
United States	9	15	13	**37**
Germany	10	13	7	**30**
Canada	14	7	5	**26**
Norway	9	8	6	**23**
Austria	4	6	6	**16**
Russia	3	5	7	**15**
South Korea	6	6	2	**14**

a battle between a stylish American and a gymnastic Russian. (For the results, see page 97.) On the women's side, a new ice queen was crowned, as South Korea's **Kim Yu-Na** set an Olympic scoring record on her way to sweeping away the gold with her amazing skills. The heartbreak story, however, was Canada's own **Joannie Rochette**. Just a few days before Joannie was set to skate, her mother passed away suddenly. Though shaken and sad, Joannie skated on and did well enough to earn a bronze medal— along with the cheers of people around the world for her courage.

The Games wrapped up with one of the biggest events in Canadian sports history. More than 80 percent of the Canadian population tuned in on the Olympics' final day to watch their team take on the United States in the gold-medal ice hockey

match. The Americans had upset Canada in an earlier round, so this was payback time. In an exciting back-and-forth match, Canada led until 24 seconds left in the game. The United States tied it with a dramatic goal that forced an overtime. In OT, Canadian **Sidney Crosby** (of the Pittsburgh Penguins) brought home the gold with a game-winner. For that game, and for all the Vancouver Games, Canada was golden.

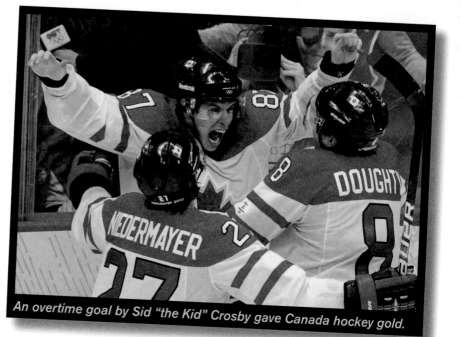

An overtime goal by Sid "the Kid" Crosby gave Canada hockey gold.

USA! USA!

Bode Miller raced through the gates into Olympic history.

win the women's downhill; she later added a bronze in the super G. **Julia Mancuso** won a pair of silver medals to go along with her gold from 2006. On the men's side, **Bode Miller** became the most decorated U.S. men's skier ever. By winning gold (combined), silver (super-G), and bronze (downhill), he brought his career total to four medals. **Andrew Weibrecht** won a surprise bronze in the super-G.

Ski Stars

The American Alpine (that means not cross-country or freestyle skiing) ski team had its greatest Winter Olympics ever! Four skiers won a total of eight medals, far and away the most by any country at this Games, and more than any other U.S. team had won in a single Olympics. **Lindsey Vonn** became the first American to

A silvery smile from skier Julia Mancuso.

Look! Up in the Air!

Freestyle skiers defy gravity by flying, flipping, and flinging through the air. American **Jeret Peterson** zoomed to a silver medal in the aerials. He landed his nearly impossible "Hurricane" trick, too. In the moguls, **Hannah Kearney** of the United States bumped and bounced to a gold, holding off hometown favorite Jennifer Heil of Canada.

Two for Gold

The sport of Nordic combined is not exactly a SportsCenter regular.

Athletes first do a ski jump, flying through the air with the greatest of ease. Back on the earth, they then take part in a cross-country ski race. It's hard work done far from the limelight. Skiers from northern European countries usually dominate. However, in Vancouver, U.S. skiers were a big surprise. **Bill Demong** won the large hill event, followed by **Johnny Spillane**. Spillane himself missed a gold in the normal hill event by only 0.4 seconds. Then the United States captured a silver medal in the team event.

Johnny Spillane leads the way in the Nordic combined race.

Golden boy: Evan Lysacek celebrates!

Evan's in Heaven!

You'd think that being the world champion in a sport would give you a big leg (or in this case, a big skate) up on winning Olympic gold. But since 1988, no reigning men's world champ has come home with gold, too . . . until Vancouver. American **Evan Lysacek** thrilled fans and judges with an elegant, flowing long program. His grace and style overcame the unique quadruple jump of highly favored defending world champion **Evgeni Plushenko** of Russia. Lysacek's joy at his success was awesome to watch; he was captured on TV, watching the scores that made him a champ come in. "I won!" he said. Yes, he did.

MORE RED, WHITE, BLUE . .

DEFYING GRAVITY ▶▶▶

Shaun White blew away the field in the half-pipe, repeating as the gold medalist. White seemed able to simply outfly the competition. The red-haired athlete known as "the Flying Tomato" stuck landing after landing with the weight of enormous expectations on his shoulders. In the women's half-pipe, Americans got silver and gold, thanks to **Hannah Teter** and **Kelly Clark**.

THE GOLDEN NIGHT TRAIN

The last time the United States won gold in the four-man bobsled was way back in 1948! That changed in Vancouver, though, as The Night Train, a U.S. sled piloted by **Steve Holcomb**, set two track records and won gold. With a half-second lead entering the last of of four trips down the track, Holcomb steered a perfect line after his teammates gave him a huge starting push. When he climbed out of the sled as an Olympic champion, thousands of supporters cheered him, cowbells ringing. Holcomb was very happy to lead his team in what had become his traditional post-race good-luck dance!

Reaching speeds above 90 mph, the U.S. bobsled team rocketed to victory!

AND GOLD

SPEEDING TO GOLD

Americans have taken part in the Winter Olympics since the Games began in 1924. Since then, no U.S. athlete has won more medals than short-track speed skater **Apollo Anton Ohno**. With his career total of eight medals, he has surpassed former record holder **Bonnie Blair**. In 2010, Ohno won two bronze medals and a silver to take over the title. In a sport famous for wild spills and crazy crashes, Ohno has battled through three Olympics to his many medals.

In long-track speed skating, American **Shani Davis** had a bit of déjà vu. Just as he did in 2006 in Torino, Davis won the 1,000 meters and finished second in the 1,500. His teammate **Chad Hedrick** was a disappointing sixth in the 1,500, but Chad rallied to help his younger teammates upset the mighty team from the Netherlands on the way to winning a silver in team pursuit.

Ohno shows his total.

NASCAR on Snow

A new Olympic sport this time around was snowboard cross. In this rock-'em-sock-'em sport, four snowboarders course down a curving track, trying to cross the finish line first without getting knocked out by their fellow racers. Falls are common, amazing jumps are part of the course, and courage is vital. U.S. racer **Seth Westscott** (right) came home with the first gold in the event, holding off a Canadian rival. Westscott was fourth in the four-man race more than halfway through, but made his way to the top with some perfectly timed jumps.

O CANADA!

Canada hosted its third Olympic Games, and its athletes loved competing in front of home crowds. The maple-leaf flag was everywhere. "O Canada" was heard more than any other anthem at the Games, too, as the nation set an Olympic record with 14 gold medals. Here's a rundown on Canada's golden champions:

TWO-PERSON LUGE (W):
Kaillie Humphries and Heather Moyse

▼▼▼ ICE DANCE:
Tessa Virtue and Scott Moir

MOGULS (M): Alexander Bilodeau

SKICROSS (W): Ashleigh McIvor

PARALLEL GIANT SLALOM (M/SNOWBOARD):
Jasey-Jay Anderson

SNOWBOARD CROSS (W): Maelle Ricker

1,000-METER SPEED SKATING (W):
Christine Nesbitt

SHORT-TRACK SKATING, 500 METERS (M):
Charles Hamelin

SKELETON (M): Jon Montgomery

5,000-METER SHORT-TRACK RELAY (M)

ICE HOCKEY (M)

ICE HOCKEY (W)

SPEED SKATING, TEAM PURSUIT (M)

CURLING (M)

MEN'S CURLING

Curling is a pretty odd sport. It's sort of like shuffleboard on ice . . . with brooms. In Canada, it's enormously popular, played by millions around the country with family and friends. The Olympic competition proved to be one of the most popular at the Games, as fans packed the arena to watch both men's and women's teams slide their stones on the "rink." Amid the pressure of performing in front of the home fans, Canada's men's team came through with the gold. They defeated Norway handily in the final, brooms flying and rocks sliding.

WORLD STARS

Canada and the United States were not the only countries in the Olympics, of course. Along with South Korea's skating star Kim Yu-Na (page 94), here are some other 2010 Winter Olympic champions of note:

ANDRE LANG, GERMANY

He won the two-man bobsled to give him a total of five gold medals, the most by anyone in the sport.

AMY WILLIAMS, GREAT BRITAIN

Great Britain is the only nation to have taken part in every Winter and Summer Olympics. Its only medal this time around came from this brave skeleton racer, who slides down the ice headfirst on her sled.

SIMON AMMAN, SWITZERLAND ▲ ▲ ▲

"The Soaring Swiss" captured both gold medals in ski jumping, one for the normal hill and one for the large hill. Of course, flying through the air off any hill isn't exactly normal! But Amman sure was large!

TORAH BRIGHT, AUSTRALIA

In Australia, are the half-pipes upside down? This wonder from Down Under held off American hopefuls Hannah Teter and Kelly Clark to bring the gold back home.

KWAME NKRUMAH-ACHEAMPONG, GHANA

He didn't win his slalom ski event (in fact, he finished next to last), but just being there was a big deal for Nkrumah-Acheampong. He was the first athlete from his country to take part in a Winter Games. In Vancouver, he earned the nickname "the Snow Leopard," after his spotted ski outfit.

NHL

HOW SWEET IT IS!

Chicago Blackhawks goalie Antti Niemi lifts the Stanley Cup after he helped his team win its first National Hockey League championship since 1961. A great Stanley Cup tradition can be seen here: Niemi's beard. NHL players traditionally do not shave during the long play-off season—for good luck. By the end of the play-offs, some teams look like squads of mountain men!

HOCKEY HIGHLIGHTS

Chicago captain Jonathan Toews (right) in action.

It was a season of young stars, record-breaking heroics, the U.S. versus Canada in an Olympic gold medal showdown (see pages 13 and 94), and the most exciting play-offs the National Hockey League has seen in a long time. By the end, the Chicago Blackhawks, one of the NHL's original six teams, won their first Stanley Cup in 49 years. There was a lot more to get excited about in 2009–10, too.

Record Setters

Phoenix Coyotes captain **Shane Doan** played his 1,000th game on December 17. Doan has played for the Coyotes (originally the Winnipeg Jets) his entire career. Another veteran record setter was New Jersey Devils goalie **Martin Brodeur**, who broke **Terry Sawchuk**'s 40-year-old record for career shutouts December 21, when he notched his 104th by blanking the Pittsburgh Penguins.

The Boston Bruins set one of the most amazing records of all. In an April 10 game against the Carolina Hurricanes, the Bruins scored three shorthanded goals in 64 seconds! It's a record that's going to be tough to beat.

Winter Classic

Watching outdoor hockey in January is pretty cold, but 38,112 fans put on their mittens and packed into Boston's Fenway Park to watch their Bruins face off against the Philadelphia Flyers in the third annual Winter Classic. The Bruins notched a 2–1 overtime victory—but they wouldn't be as lucky when they faced the Flyers in the play-offs three months later.

Youth Movement

The NHL has a bunch of exciting young stars who shined brightly in 2009–10. Buffalo Sabres defenseman **Tyler Myers**, Colorado Avalanche center **Matt Duchene**, and Detroit Red Wings goalie **Jimmy Howard** were nominated for the Calder Trophy (rookie of the year). In his second season, 20-year-old Tampa Bay Lightning forward **Steven Stamkos** finished the season tied with the Penguins' **Sidney Crosby** for the most goals (51). And the Los Angeles Kings were led to their first play-off appearance in eight years by a trio of youngsters: center **Anze Kopitar**, defenseman **Drew Doughty**, and goalie **Jonathan Quick**.

Some of the game's youngest players showed their best in the play-offs, including **Claude Giroux**, **Mike Richards**, and **Ville Leino** for the Flyers. Speedy **P. K. Subban** of the Montreal Canadiens and **Joe Pavelski** of the San Jose Sharks were constant threats on the ice.

Kopitar leads a pack of young stars.

FINAL STANDINGS

EASTERN CONFERENCE	PTS
*Washington **Capitals**	121
*New Jersey **Devils**	103
*Buffalo **Sabres**	100
Pittsburgh **Penguins**	101
Ottawa **Senators**	94
Boston **Bruins**	91
Philadelphia **Flyers**	88
Montreal **Canadiens**	88
New York **Rangers**	87
Atlanta **Thrashers**	83
Carolina **Hurricanes**	80
Tampa Bay **Lightning**	80
New York **Islanders**	79
Florida **Panthers**	77
Toronto **Maple Leafs**	74

WESTERN CONFERENCE	PTS
*San Jose **Sharks**	113
*Chicago **Blackhawks**	112
*Vancouver **Canucks**	103
Phoenix **Coyotes**	107
Detroit **Red Wings**	102
Los Angeles **Kings**	101
Nashville **Predators**	100
Colorado **Avalanche**	95
St. Louis **Blues**	90
Calgary **Flames**	90
Anaheim **Ducks**	89
Dallas **Stars**	88
Minnesota **Wild**	84
Columbus **Blue Jackets**	79
Edmonton **Oilers**	62

*Division winners

Patrick Kane (top center) scores to give Chicago its first Stanley Cup since 1961.

STANLEY CUP PLAY-OFFS

One of the most thrilling Stanley Cup play-offs ever ended when **Patrick Kane** of the Chicago Blackhawks slipped a shot through the legs of Philadelphia Flyers goalie **Michael Leighton** in overtime in Game 6. The goal gave the Blackhawks their first Stanley Cup since 1961.

There were many new faces in the 2010 play-offs. The Los Angeles Kings and the Phoenix Coyotes returned to postseason play after eight years of missing out. The Kings lost a hard-fought first-round series to the Vancouver Canucks in six games. The Coyotes faced off against the veteran Detroit Red Wings and battled heroically before getting knocked out in seven games.

The biggest spoilers were the Montreal Canadiens. In the first round they faced the Washington Capitals, the team with the NHL's best record. Led by the spectacular goaltending of 25-year-old **Jaroslav Halak**, the Canadiens eliminated the Capitals in Game 7. For an encore, they faced the defending champion Pittsburgh Penguins in the next round. Once again, Halak was a wall and the Canadiens sent **Sidney Crosby** and company home in seven games.

In the conference semifinals, the Philadelphia Flyers fell behind the Boston Bruins three games to none. Only two other teams in NHL history have come back from a 3–0 hole, but the Flyers battled back and took Game 7 on Boston's home ice.

The Stanley Cup Finals pitted the hard-hitting Flyers against the speedy Blackhawks. The series began in Chicago with a wild 6–5 Blackhawks win in which the lead changed five times. Game 2 went to the Blackhawks, and Game 3 seemed to be headed that way until Flyers forward **Ville Leino** tied it. It finally ended with **Claude Giroux** tipping in a shot in overtime to give the Flyers the win.

The Flyers won Game 4, 4–3. Game 5 saw the Blackhawks use their muscle and skill to dominate with a 7–4 win.

Game 6 was a classic. The teams swapped power-play goals and the score was 1–1 at the end of the first period. The Flyers jumped to a 2–1 lead when **Danny Briere** fired the puck into the top of the net. Flyers fans were going crazy, but the Blackhawks fought back and ended the second period with a 3–2 lead. With 3:59 left to play, the Flyers' **Scott Hartnell** knocked in a loose puck to send the game to overtime. The Flyers almost scored immediately into the overtime, but Chicago goalie **Antti Niemi** made a huge save. The Blackhawks then went on the attack. Kane cut around a Flyers defender and snapped the puck past Leighton to win the Cup.

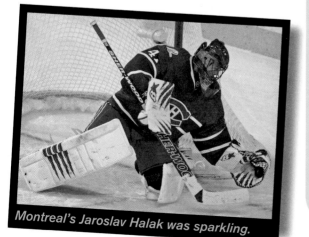
Montreal's Jaroslav Halak was sparkling.

PLAY-OFF RESULTS
(Games won in parentheses)

FIRST ROUND

EASTERN CONFERENCE
Montreal OVER Washington (4-3)
Pittsburgh OVER Ottawa (4-2)
Philadelphia OVER New Jersey (4-1)
Boston OVER Buffalo (4-2)

WESTERN CONFERENCE
San Jose OVER Colorado (4-2)
Detroit OVER Phoenix (4-3)
Vancouver OVER Los Angeles (4-2)
Chicago OVER Nashville (4-2)

CONFERENCE SEMIFINALS

EASTERN CONFERENCE
Montreal OVER Pittsburgh (4-3)
Philadelphia OVER Boston (4-3)

WESTERN CONFERENCE
San Jose OVER Detroit (4-1)
Chicago OVER Vancouver (4-2)

CONFERENCE FINALS

EASTERN CONFERENCE
Philadelphia OVER Montreal (4-1)

WESTERN CONFERENCE
Chicago OVER San Jose (4-0)

STANLEY CUP FINALS
Chicago OVER Philadelphia (4-2)

2009-10 AWARDS

Stanley Cup
CHICAGO BLACKHAWKS

Conn Smythe Trophy
(Stanley Cup Play-offs MVP)
JONATHAN TOEWS,
Chicago Blackhawks

Clarence Campbell Bowl
(Western Conference champions)
CHICAGO BLACKHAWKS

Prince of Wales Trophy
(Eastern Conference champions)
PHILADELPHIA FLYERS

President's Trophy
(best regular-season record: 121 points)
WASHINGTON CAPITALS

Hart Trophy (MVP)
◄◄◄HENRIK SEDIN,
Vancouver Canucks

Ted Lindsay Award
(outstanding player as voted by the players)
ALEXANDER OVECHKIN,
Washington Capitals

Vezina Trophy (best goaltender)
RYAN MILLER, Buffalo Sabres

James Norris Memorial Trophy
(best defenseman)
DUNCAN KEITH, Chicago Blackhawks

Calder Memorial Trophy (best rookie)
TYLER MYERS, Buffalo Sabres

Art Ross Trophy (top point scorer)
HENRIK SEDIN, Vancouver Canucks,
29 goals, 83 assists, 112 points

Maurice Richard Trophy
(top goal scorer)
SIDNEY CROSBY,
Pittsburgh Penguins, 51 goals
STEVEN STAMKOS,
Tampa Bay Lightning, 51 goals

Lady Byng Memorial Trophy
(most gentlemanly player)
MARTIN ST. LOUIS,
Tampa Bay Lightning

UP AHEAD ON THE ICE

◎ NHL IN EUROPE

European fans are going to get a look at NHL hockey when six teams open their seasons in three European cities. The Carolina Hurricanes and Minnesota Wild will face off for two games in Helsinki, Finland. Fans in Stockholm, Sweden, will get to see the Columbus Blue Jackets battle the San Jose Sharks in two contests, and the Boston Bruins will take on the Phoenix Coyotes for two games in Prague, Czech Republic. "I think it's going to be a great experience to go back and play in your home country," says Hurricanes defenseman **Joni Pitkanen** of Finland.

◎ WINTER CLASSIC

The NFL's Steelers won't be the team wearing black and gold on Pittsburgh's Heinz Field in January 2011. The fourth annual Winter Classic will take place at the Steelers' stadium on New Year's Day. The Penguins will be the home team when they play the Washington Capitals. There's more outdoor hockey when McMahon Stadium in Calgary, Alberta, sets up a rink for the second Heritage Classic. The hometown Flames will rumble with the Montreal Canadiens in what promises to be a chilly but fun February 20 contest.

SCANDINAVIAN STARS

The NHL has players from every corner of the globe, but stars from Scandinavian countries made a huge impact in 2009–10, especially in the play-offs. Many of the top goalies were from Finland: the Bruins' **Tuukka Rask**, the Predators' **Pekka Rinne**, and the Stanley Cup champion Blackhawks' **Antti Niemi**. Sweden also had its share of standouts, including Red Wings forwards **Johan Franzen** and **Henrik Zetterberg**, Canucks forwards **Henrik** and **Daniel Sedin** and **Mikael Samuelsson**, and Blackhawks defenseman **Niklas Hjalmarsson**.

After the Blackhawks won the Cup, Hjalmarsson said, "My town in Sweden has 90 people. They watch tonight's game at two in the morning, then go milk cows at five. They are more tired than I am. Wait until I bring the Cup there—they will not be tired."

Boston's goalie Tuukka Rask is one of Finland's best, too.

STANLEY CUP CHAMPIONS

2009–10	**Chicago Blackhawks**		1983–84	**Edmonton Oilers**
2008–09	**Pittsburgh Penguins**		1982–83	**New York Islanders**
2007–08	**Detroit Red Wings**		1981–82	**New York Islanders**
2006–07	**Anaheim Ducks**		1980–81	**New York Islanders**
2005–06	**Carolina Hurricanes**		1979–80	**New York Islanders**
2004–05	No champion (Lockout)		1978–79	**Montreal Canadiens**
2003–04	**Tampa Bay Lightning**		1977–78	**Montreal Canadiens**
2002–03	**New Jersey Devils**		1976–77	**Montreal Canadiens**
2001–02	**Detroit Red Wings**		1975–76	**Montreal Canadiens**
2000–01	**Colorado Avalanche**		1974–75	**Philadelphia Flyers**
1999–00	**New Jersey Devils**		1973–74	**Philadelphia Flyers**
1998–99	**Dallas Stars**		1972–73	**Montreal Canadiens**
1997–98	**Detroit Red Wings**		1971–72	**Boston Bruins**
1996–97	**Detroit Red Wings**		1970–71	**Montreal Canadiens**
1995–96	**Colorado Avalanche**		1969–70	**Boston Bruins**
1994–95	**New Jersey Devils**		1968–69	**Montreal Canadiens**
1993–94	**New York Rangers**		1967–68	**Montreal Canadiens**
1992–93	**Montreal Canadiens**		1966–67	**Toronto Maple Leafs**
1991–92	**Pittsburgh Penguins**		1965–66	**Montreal Canadiens**
1990–91	**Pittsburgh Penguins**		1964–65	**Montreal Canadiens**
1989–90	**Edmonton Oilers**		1963–64	**Toronto Maple Leafs**
1988–89	**Calgary Flames**		1962–63	**Toronto Maple Leafs**
1987–88	**Edmonton Oilers**		1961–62	**Toronto Maple Leafs**
1986–87	**Edmonton Oilers**		1960–61	**Chicago Blackhawks**
1985–86	**Montreal Canadiens**		1959–60	**Montreal Canadiens**
1984–85	**Edmonton Oilers**		1958–59	**Montreal Canadiens**

1957–58	**Montreal Canadiens**
1956–57	**Montreal Canadiens**
1955–56	**Montreal Canadiens**
1954–55	**Detroit Red Wings**
1953–54	**Detroit Red Wings**
1952–53	**Montreal Canadiens**
1951–52	**Detroit Red Wings**
1950–51	**Toronto Maple Leafs**
1949–50	**Detroit Red Wings**
1948–49	**Toronto Maple Leafs**
1947–48	**Toronto Maple Leafs**
1946–47	**Toronto Maple Leafs**
1945–46	**Montreal Canadiens**
1944–45	**Toronto Maple Leafs**
1943–44	**Montreal Canadiens**
1942–43	**Detroit Red Wings**
1941–42	**Toronto Maple Leafs**
1940–41	**Boston Bruins**
1939–40	**New York Rangers**
1938–39	**Boston Bruins**
1937–38	**Chicago Blackhawks**
1936–37	**Detroit Red Wings**
1935–36	**Detroit Red Wings**
1934–35	**Montreal Maroons**
1933–34	**Chicago Blackhawks**
1932–33	**New York Rangers**
1931–32	**Toronto Maple Leafs**
1930–31	**Montreal Canadiens**
1929–30	**Montreal Canadiens**

Wayne Gretzky's Oilers won five Stanley Cups.

1928–29	**Boston Bruins**
1927–28	**New York Rangers**
1926–27	**Ottawa Senators**
1925–26	**Montreal Maroons**
1924–25	**Victoria Cougars**
1923–24	**Montreal Canadiens**
1922–23	**Ottawa Senators**
1921–22	**Toronto St. Pats**
1920–21	**Ottawa Senators**
1919–20	**Ottawa Senators**
1918–19	No decision
1917–18	**Toronto Arenas**

NASCAR

TRAFFIC JAM!
The racing was fast and furious at the Aaron's 499 at the Talladega Superspeedway in Alabama in the spring of 2010. This nine-car wreck ruined the afternoon for some drivers, but not for Kevin Harvick, who won one of the most dramatic races in NASCAR history (see page 118).

NO. 4 FOR NO. 48!

Jimmie Johnson's crew is a whirlwind of activity during a race-day pit stop.

Even before the season-ending Ford 400 at the Homestead-Miami Speedway, the winner of NASCAR's 2009 Sprint Cup was a "four-gone" conclusion. That's because Jimmie Johnson, the three-time defending champion, charged to the front of the pack early in the Chase race and easily won the title again.

NASCAR instituted its "Chase for the Cup" format in 2004. It hoped that the play-off-like Chase would generate

> **The truth of it is, to do something that's never been done in this sport . . . is so awesome!**
>
> — JIMMIE JOHNSON

added excitement and keep fans and drivers guessing who would win right down to the final laps of the season. Most years, it's worked. But 2009 was not most years.

With history in his grasp—no driver had ever won four consecutive NASCAR season points championships—Johnson took the overall lead in the standings in the fourth race of the ten-race Chase, and he never let go. Johnson and his No. 48 car won four Chase races, and finished second, fourth, fifth, sixth, and ninth in five others. His lone stumble came at the Dickies 500 in Texas in the third-to-last race, when he was involved in a wreck, couldn't finish, and placed 38th.

Needing only a 25th-place finish going into the last race, Johnson finished fifth in the Ford 400 to coast to the title 141 points ahead of second-place Mark Martin. Jeff Gordon (Johnson's teammate at Hendrick Motorsports and a four-time career champion himself—just not in a row) finished third, but a distant 179 points behind.

For Martin, it was a bittersweet season: He had a terrific year but still fell short of the season points championship that has eluded him his entire career (which began in 1981). Martin's career was supposed to be winding down when he began driving partial-race schedules in 2007 and 2008. But in 2009, at age 50, he drove the full 36-race schedule and notched his fifth runner-up finish in the season standings. It was the 17th time he had placed in the top 10.

Martin was back for more in 2010, and he started on the pole for the season-opening Daytona 500 before finishing 12th. Jamie McMurray won that race in his first start with the Earnhardt Ganassi Racing team after several disappointing seasons with Roush Racing.

McMurray's win was a feel-good story, although this was not true for other drivers in 2010:

Popular Mark Martin is still in search of his first season title.

Tempers flared early and often. This was due in part to a change in the rules that allowed for more bumping.

There was another big rules change, too: Early in the season, NASCAR removed the "wing" on the backs of the cars and put a spoiler back on. In 2007, after more than 40 years, the spoiler had been removed. The idea was that the wing would make racing safer for drivers because the cars would handle better. But NASCAR discovered that the cars actually handled better with the spoiler. That meant more aggressive racing. And that promised to bring lots of excitement for drivers and fans throughout the 2010 season!

CHASE FOR THE CUP
2009 FINAL STANDINGS

	DRIVER	POINTS
1.	Jimmie JOHNSON	6,652
2.	Mark MARTIN	6,511
3.	Jeff GORDON	6,473
4.	Kurt BUSCH	6,446
5.	Denny HAMLIN	6,335
6.	Tony STEWART	6,309
7.	Greg BIFFLE	6,292
8.	Juan Pablo MONTOYA	6,252
9.	Ryan NEWMAN	6,175
10.	Kasey KAHNE	6,128
11.	Carl EDWARDS	6,118
12.	Brian VICKERS	5,929

MEET THE DRIVERS!

Denny Hamlin crosses the finish line ahead of the pack at the Pocono Raceway in June 2010.

JIMMIE JOHNSON

Jimmie Johnson's place as one of the greatest drivers in NASCAR history is already secure. He's the only man ever to win four Cup series titles in a row. Only Richard Petty and Dale Earnhardt Sr. (with seven each) have ever won more career championships. And when Johnson won his 50th career race at Bristol early in 2010, he equaled the legendary Junior Johnson and Ned Jarrett for No. 10 on NASCAR's all-time wins list.

What's left to prove? Well, after the spoiler was put back on the car in 2010, Johnson finished 10th or lower five times in his next eight starts. Critics started to whisper that maybe Johnson had simply figured out how to race with the wing quicker than the other drivers, and that now his championship reign was over. Those whispers just might be enough incentive for Johnson to prove the critics wrong and win a fifth consecutive Cup championship.

DENNY HAMLIN

Not even a torn ligament in his knee could stop Denny Hamlin early in the 2010 season. (It must be painful to sit in a race car for hours with that injury!) He simply had surgery to fix it, then was back behind the wheel 10 days later. Hamlin won the first race with the spoiler back on the car, at the short track in Martinsville in March. Three weeks later, he won at the long track in Texas. After a fifth-place overall finish in 2009, Hamlin won 5 of his first 16 starts in 2010 and also posted 4 other top-five finishes. This tough, young driver is poised to become a yearly challenger for the Cup title.

JEFF **GORDON**

Maybe no other driver was as happy about the change back to the spoiler from the wing as **Jeff Gordon** was. That's because Gordon won 79 Cup races with a spoiler on his No. 24 car, but only 3 races with the wing. He won four season titles with the spoiler, but none with the wing. With the spoiler back on, Gordon quickly began reeling off top-10 race finishes. He appears on the verge of regaining the form that made him NASCAR's most successful driver of the late 1990s and early 2000s.

Jeff Gordon eyes a return to the top.

JUAN PABLO **MONTOYA**

Like most drivers who cross over from open-wheel racing, **Juan Pablo Montoya** took a little time to get up to speed. But the former Indianapolis 500 champ has proved he has the ability to compete for the Sprint Cup title. In 2009, he made the Chase for the Cup. Then he placed fourth or better in five of the first six Chase races, before falling back and finishing eighth in the standings.

Nationwide & Camping World Truck Series

The lines between NASCAR's top racing classes have blurred in recent seasons as more and more Sprint Cup stars are also driving in the Nationwide and Camping World Truck series. (Hey, these guys just love to race!)

The Nationwide series features cars that are a little lighter and less powerful than NASCAR's top series. Sprint Cup star **Kyle Busch** won the Nationwide title for 2009. In 2010, **Brad Keselowski** got off to a hot start, with 10 top-five finishes in the first 13 races.

The Camping World Truck series features drivers racing . . . trucks, of course! **Ron Hornaday Sr.** is as close as anyone comes to being the Jimmie Johnson of the Camping World Truck series. Hornaday Sr. won the 2007 championship, finished only seven points behind in 2008, then returned to the top in 2009. Not surprisingly, he was among the leaders early in 2010, too.

Ron Hornaday Sr. is a star driver in the truck series.

AROUND THE TRACK

McMurray's Big Win

Jamie McMurray looked in his rearview mirror and saw **Dale Earnhardt Jr.** charging . . . fast! It was the last lap of the Daytona 500—a race that had been delayed several times by a pothole in the road!—and McMurray was clinging to the lead. McMurray put the pedal to the metal and held off Earnhardt to win NASCAR's most famous race for the first time in his career.

Double Duty for Danica ▲

For years, fans have wondered if **Danica Patrick** was going to make the leap from open-wheel IndyCar racing to NASCAR. Well, she didn't exactly jump into the stock car pool in 2010, but she did dip her toes in. Danica, whose crossover appeal has made her a star with racing fans and nonfans alike, drove several races in the Nationwide Series in 2010. In her first three starts, she finished 35th, 31st, and 36th. As they say, it really was a learning experience!

Tradin' Paint at Talladega

The Talladega Superspeedway has produced some of the most exciting races in NASCAR history, but the Aaron's 499 in April of 2010 may have been the best of them all. Amazingly, a record 29 different drivers led the race at one time or another. (Only 43 drivers are entered in a Cup Series race.) The lead changed hands 89 times in all, another record. **Kevin Harvick** led only two laps the entire race, but one was the most important—the last one! Harvick dipped under Jamie McMurray to pass on the last turn of the last lap and won by 0.011 seconds. That's 11 one-thousandths of one second!

Calm Down, Fellas ▶

There was a lot of pushing and shoving (among the stock cars, we mean) on NASCAR tracks early in the 2010 season . . . even a little more than usual. That led to some flaring tempers. Like the time in Atlanta when Carl Edwards bumped Brad Keselowski from behind and inadvertently sent Keselowski's car flying. Luckily, Keselowski wasn't hurt. However, the incident set up a summer-long series of confrontations between the two drivers.

Harvick (No. 29) and Logano (No. 20) tangled.

At the Pocono Raceway in June, Kevin Harvick and Joey Logano got into a war of words after a bump from Harvick sent Logano's car into the wall. And even the normally mild-mannered Jeff Gordon was upset after he tangled with teammate Jimmie Johnson on the track in one race. "It takes a lot to make me mad," Gordon said. "And I am mad right now."

2010 NASCAR CHAMPION

We don't know the 2010 champ because this book had to print before the season was over. So we'll take our best guess here. The easy thing to do, of course, would be to pick Jimmie Johnson to win it all yet again. But no one can win it every year, right? Besides, there are a lot of other NASCAR drivers who are ready for their turn in the spotlight. You've read about a few of them on the previous pages. Our prediction for the 2010 Chase for the Cup champion is:

★ Kyle Busch ★

Kyle's brother Kurt was the 2004 NASCAR champ. We think that this year it's little brother's turn.

NASCAR CHAMPIONS

Year	Driver	Make		Year	Driver	Make
2009	Jimmie Johnson	Chevrolet		1990	Dale Earnhardt Sr.	Chevrolet
2008	Jimmie Johnson	Chevrolet		1989	Rusty Wallace	Pontiac
2007	Jimmie Johnson	Chevrolet		1988	Bill Elliott	Ford
2006	Jimmie Johnson	Chevrolet		1987	Dale Earnhardt Sr.	Chevrolet
2005	Tony Stewart	Chevrolet		1986	Dale Earnhardt Sr.	Chevrolet
2004	Kurt Busch	Ford		1985	Darrell Waltrip	Chevrolet
2003	Matt Kenseth	Ford		1984	Terry Labonte	Chevrolet
2002	Tony Stewart	Pontiac		1983	Bobby Allison	Buick
2001	Jeff Gordon	Chevrolet		1982	Darrell Waltrip	Buick
2000	Bobby Labonte	Pontiac		1981	Darrell Waltrip	Buick
1999	Dale Jarrett	Ford		1980	Dale Earnhardt Sr.	Chevrolet
1998	Jeff Gordon	Chevrolet		1979	Richard Petty	Chevrolet
1997	Jeff Gordon	Chevrolet		1978	Cale Yarborough	Oldsmobile
1996	Terry Labonte	Chevrolet		1977	Cale Yarborough	Chevrolet
1995	Jeff Gordon	Chevrolet		1976	Cale Yarborough	Chevrolet
1994	Dale Earnhardt Sr.	Chevrolet		1975	Richard Petty	Dodge
1993	Dale Earnhardt Sr.	Chevrolet		1974	Richard Petty	Dodge
1992	Alan Kulwicki	Ford		1973	Benny Parsons	Chevrolet
1991	Dale Earnhardt Sr.	Chevrolet		1972	Richard Petty	Plymouth

1971	Richard Petty	Plymouth
1970	Bobby Isaac	Dodge
1969	David Pearson	Ford
1968	David Pearson	Ford
1967	Richard Petty	Plymouth
1966	David Pearson	Dodge
1965	Ned Jarrett	Ford
1964	Richard Petty	Plymouth
1963	Joe Weatherly	Pontiac
1962	Joe Weatherly	Pontiac
1961	Ned Jarrett	Chevrolet
1960	Rex White	Chevrolet
1959	Lee Petty	Plymouth
1958	Lee Petty	Oldsmobile
1957	Buck Baker	Chevrolet
1956	Buck Baker	Chrysler
1955	Tim Flock	Chrysler
1954	Lee Petty	Chrysler
1953	Herb Thomas	Hudson
1952	Tim Flock	Hudson
1951	Herb Thomas	Hudson
1950	Bill Rexford	Oldsmobile
1949	Red Byron	Oldsmobile

NASCAR'S WINNINGEST DRIVERS

(career Cup Series victories entering 2010)

DRIVER	RACES WON	DRIVER	RACES WON
1. Richard PETTY	200	7. Dale EARNHARDT Sr.	76
2. David PEARSON	105	8. Rusty WALLACE	55
3. Bobby ALLISON	84	9. Lee PETTY	54
Darrell WALTRIP	84	10. Ned JARRETT	50
5. Cale YARBOROUGH	83	Junior JOHNSON	50
6. Jeff GORDON	82		

OTHER MOTOR SPORTS

LEADER OF THE PACK

That's Dario Franchitti in the No. 10 car, out front at the Indianapolis 500 in May of 2010. Franchitti went on to win the most important event on the IndyCar schedule for the second time in his career.

OPEN-WHEEL RACING

◀◀◀ Super Dario!

After a lost season in stock cars, **Dario Franchitti** made a triumphant return to open-wheel racing in 2009. The 2007 Indy Racing League season champion won the IRL points title again in 2009.

Franchitti spent the 2008 season racing in NASCAR—part of the season, anyway. In 10 starts, he posted an average finish of 34th place before owner **Chip Ganassi** disbanded the No. 40 team, citing a lack of sponsorship. Back in the IRL in 2009, Franchitti finished fourth in the season-opening race at St. Petersburg, Florida, then won his very next time out, in the Grand Prix through the streets of Long Beach, California.

Franchitti won four more times on the 17-race schedule, with the last victory coming in the season finale in Homestead, Florida. That let him edge Chip Ganassi Racing teammate **Scott Dixon** by 11 points, with Penske Racing's **Ryan Briscoe** another point behind. All three drivers had had a chance to win the season title going into the last race.

Ganassi's Double

When **Dario Franchitti** won the Indianapolis 500 in May of 2010, it completed a unique double for car owner **Chip Ganassi**. He became the first owner ever with the winning car in both the Daytona 500 (the biggest race on the NASCAR schedule) and the Indianapolis 500 (the biggest race on the IndyCar circuit) in the same season. In February, **Jamie McMurray** won the Daytona 500 while driving for the Earnhardt Ganassi Racing team.

2009 IRL FINAL STANDINGS

DRIVER	POINTS
1. Dario FRANCHITTI	616
2. Scott DIXON	605
3. Ryan BRISCOE	604
4. Helio CASTRONEVES	433
5. Danica PATRICK	393

Button after clinching the season title.

2009 F1 FINAL STANDINGS

DRIVER	POINTS
1. Jenson BUTTON	95.0
2. Sebastian VETTEL	84.0
3. Rubens BARRICHELLO	77.0
4. Mark WEBBER	69.5
5. Lewis HAMILTON	49.0

F1 CHAMP

Englishman **Jenson Button** won 6 of the 17 races on the schedule to win the Formula One World Drivers Championship for 2009. Button's first career title came on the heels of fellow countryman Lewis Hamilton's win in 2008. It marked the first time in Formula One's 60-year history that English drivers had won the championship in back-to-back seasons.

No American squads competed in the 10-team Formula One World Championship for 2009 (which was also the first season in which no races were held in the United States or Canada). When the circuit expanded to 13 teams for the 2010 season, an American team, USF1, was slated to take part. But USF1 never made it to the starting grid, and it eventually disbanded.

New for 2010: Push to Pass ▶▶▶

Push a button and make the car go faster. Sounds like a video game, right? Actually, it's a high-tech gadget that has been used in open-wheel racing before but made its full-time debut in the Indy Racing League in 2010. The "Push to Pass" button gives drivers an extra boost of horsepower when they need to make a move on the track. The trick is that drivers can only use Push to Pass a certain number of times (it varies) in a race, so strategy is really important.

The combination of Push to Pass and the lone short track on the IndyCar schedule made for one of the IRL's most exciting races at the Iowa Speedway in June of 2010. **Tony Kanaan** passed race leader **Helio Castroneves** 10 laps from the end and went on to win.

DRAGSTER CHAMPIONS

Six for Schu ▲

Tony Schumacher (in the dragster at the top of the photo above) won the National Hot Rod Association (NHRA) Top Fuel season championship for 2009. Top Fuel is the drag racing class that features the most powerful engines. It was the sixth consecutive title for Schumacher.

Schumacher entered 2009 with a new crew chief, **Mike Green**. Schumacher's previous crew chief, **Alan Johnson**, had left to start his own team with rival **Larry Dixon** as the driver. Schumacher and Dixon were among the four different drivers to win the first 4 Top Fuel events on the 2009 schedule, and among the eight to win the 24 events in all. In the end, Schumacher held off Dixon by only two points to win.

The two drivers were back at it again in 2010. Dixon got off to a quick start by winning the season-opening event in Pomona, California. Midway through the season, he still held the edge over Schumacher, who was in second place.

Family Affair

Robert Hight won NHRA's Funny Car division for the first time, but it was not without controversy. One of Hight's fellow racers alleged that there was, well . . . some funny business going on.

Here's what happened: Hight beat Funny Car legend **John Force** in the semifinal round at the U.S. Nationals to earn a spot in the "Countdown to 1" play-offs—and to lock out 2008 champ **Cruz Pedregon** from those play-offs. That led to a heated exchange between Force and **Tony Pedregon** (Cruz's brother), which was caught by television cameras. Pedregon felt that Force, who had already qualified for the Countdown, had not tried his best to beat Hight—who is Force's son-in-law. The two men nearly came to blows.

After barely making it into the Countdown, Hight eventually went on to win the season championship. Still, there was an ironic twist: Hight's Countdown performance kept **Ashley Force Hood**, Force's daughter and the Funny Car runner-up in 2009, from winning her first championship.

A Long Time Coming

Mike Edwards won the NHRA's Pro Stock season championship, easily outdistancing three-time champion **Greg Anderson**, who finished in second place.

It was the 52-year-old Edwards's second national title, after the NHRA Modified championship that he won . . . in 1981! That's right, it was a record 28 years in between titles for Edwards.

Edwards waited a long time for this.

SEASON STANDINGS

TOP FUEL

DRIVER	POINTS
1. Tony SCHUMACHER	2,571
2. Larry DIXON	2,569
3. Antron BROWN	2,522
4. Cory McCLENATHAN	2,490
5. Brandon BERNSTEIN	2,438

FUNNY CAR

DRIVER	POINTS
1. Robert HIGHT	2,547
2. Ashley FORCE HOOD	2,481
3. Ron CAPPS	2,433
4. Tim WILKERSON	2,430
5. Jack BECKMAN	2,406

PRO STOCK

DRIVER	POINTS
1. Mike EDWARDS	2,682
2. Greg ANDERSON	2,572
3. Jason LINE	2,486
4. Greg STANFIELD	2,403
5. Jeg COUGHLIN Jr.	2,375

MOTOCROSS/SUPERCROSS

Vegas. He left little doubt about the outcome, bursting from the gate to take his fifth hole shot of the season. (The hole shot is the rider who comes out of the first turn with the lead.) He went on to lead all 20 laps in the race. It capped a breakout year for Dungey, who also won the Lites division in the outdoor AMA motocross season for 2009.

◀◀◀Girl Power

Ashley Fiolek first garnered attention because she's deaf—and because she didn't let that stop her from racing in competition. But her deafness is just a footnote to her career now. Instead, she's known as a champion rider after winning the season title in women's motocross (WMX) for 2009.

Fiolek entered the last race in Delmont, Pennsylvania, needing to finish only 11th or better on her Honda to clinch the championship. But midway through the race, she crashed on the back side of a tabletop jump. Despite severe pain in her collarbone, she got back on her bike and completed the race, finishing in seventh place to clinch the title. It was only later that she found out she had broken her collarbone in the crash.

A New Star

Ryan Dungey rode a Suzuki to his first American Motorcyclist Association (AMA) supercross championship in 2010. (The AMA's supercross schedule runs from January to May.) The 20-year-old from Eden Prairie, Minnesota, won 6 of the 17 events on the supercross schedule, including the season finale in Las

Tough Breaks

Ryan Dungey emerged as a breakout star in supercross and motocross, but where were the other big names, such as **James "Bubba" Stewart** and **Chad Reed**? Both were slowed by injuries in 2010—although not before escalating their longtime rivalry.

Early in the 2010 season, the pair got tangled on the track during the final lap of a race in Phoenix. In the accident, Stewart broke a bone in his wrist and Reed broke his hand. Stewart raced the next week in Anaheim, then had surgery and missed the rest of the season. Reed didn't come back until late in the season.

EVERYTHING ON WHEELS
(AND MORE!)

◀ **Hector Arana**, 52, won the NHRA's Pro Stock Motorcycle season championship for the first time in 2009. Pro Stock Motorcycle is a popular division of drag racing events. Of course, you can put two of just about any motorized vehicle on a track and folks are going to love racing them. Here are just a few of the many (way too many to list all of them!) other motor sports events on wheels—and snow, and water . . .

✱ Lawn mowers: The United States Lawn Mower Racing Association (USLMRA) calls itself America's "Grass Roots" motor sport! It hosted the inaugural U.S. Open in September of 2010 in Delaware, Ohio.

✱ Monster trucks: **Larry Swim** of Bigfoot #14 (Bigfoot Bad Boy) earned Driver of the Year honors from the Monster Truck Racing Association. Swim and his truck won 19 races in 2009.

✱ Powerboats: Italy's **Guido Cappellini** won the F1 Powerboat World Championship in 2009. It was his 10th win in 17 years, but his first since 2005. ▶

✱ Snowmobiles: **Matt Schulz** won the 2010 World Championship Snowmobile Derby. Since 1964, the event has been held each January in Eagle River, Wisconsin.

MAJOR CHAMPIONS
OF THE 2000s

TOP FUEL DRAGSTERS

YEAR	DRIVER
2009	Tony Schumacher
2008	Tony Schumacher
2007	Tony Schumacher
2006	Tony Schumacher
2005	Tony Schumacher
2004	Tony Schumacher
2003	Larry Dixon
2002	Larry Dixon
2001	Kenny Bernstein
2000	Gary Scelzi

Two-time Funny Car champ Tony Pedregon

FUNNY CARS

YEAR	DRIVER
2009	Robert Hight
2008	Cruz Pedregon
2007	Tony Pedregon

2006	John Force
2005	Gary Scelzi
2004	John Force
2003	Tony Pedregon
2002	John Force
2001	John Force
2000	John Force

PRO STOCK CARS

YEAR	DRIVER
2009	Mike Edwards
2008	Jeg Coughlin Jr.
2007	Jeg Coughlin Jr.
2006	Jason Line
2005	Greg Anderson
2004	Greg Anderson
2003	Greg Anderson
2002	Jeg Coughlin Jr.
2001	Warren Johnson
2000	Jeg Coughlin Jr.

FORMULA 1

YEAR	DRIVER
2009	Jenson Button
2008	Lewis Hamilton
2007	Kimi Raikkonen
2006	Fernando Alonso

2005	Fernando Alonso
2004	Michael Schumacher
2003	Michael Schumacher
2002	Michael Schumacher
2001	Michael Schumacher
2000	Michael Schumacher

INDY RACING LEAGUE

YEAR	DRIVER
2009	Dario Franchitti
2008	Scott Dixon
2007	Dario Franchitti
2006	Sam Hornish Jr. and Dan Wheldon (tie)
2005	Dan Wheldon
2004	Tony Kanaan
2003	Scott Dixon
2002	Sam Hornish Jr.

| 2001 | Sam Hornish Jr. |
| 2000 | Buddy Lazier |

AMA SUPERCROSS

YEAR	DRIVER
2010	Ryan Dungey
2009	James Stewart Jr.
2008	Chad Reed
2007	James Stewart Jr.
2006	Ricky Carmichael
2005	Ricky Carmichael
2004	Chad Reed
2003	Ricky Carmichael
2002	Ricky Carmichael
2001	Ricky Carmichael
2000	Jeremy McGrath

AMA MOTOCROSS

YEAR	RIDER (MOTOCROSS)	RIDER (LITES)
2009	Chad Reed	Ryan Dungey
2008	James Stewart Jr.	Ryan Villopoto
2007	Grant Langston	Ryan Villopoto
2006	Ricky Carmichael	Ryan Villopoto
2005	Ricky Carmichael	Ivan Tedesco
2004	Ricky Carmichael	James Stewart Jr.
2003	Ricky Carmichael	Grant Langston
2002	Ricky Carmichael	James Stewart Jr.
2001	Ricky Carmichael	Mike Brown
2000	Ricky Carmichael	Travis Pastrana

Ryan Villopoto

ACTION SPORTS

UP, UP, AND AWAY!
Extreme sports star Travis Pastrana climbs a wall on his motocross bike during a stunt in the freestyle competition at the 2010 Summer X Games in Los Angeles. Pastrana put an exclamation point on his gold medal in this event by doing a double backflip (see page 137).

2009-2010 WRAP-UP

He's Baaack!

The year marked the return of extreme sports legend **Shaun White**. Okay, the truth is, White hadn't really gone anywhere, but he ramped up his schedule again in 2010.

White might seem like he's everywhere to folks who aren't extreme sports fans. In 2010, White began the year by competing in the Winter X Games in Aspen, and then the Winter Olympics in Vancouver. Then it was on to the Summer X Games in Los Angeles and a return to the Dew Tour in skateboarding for the first time since 2008.

At the ripe "old" age of 23, White showed he's still got it, too. He won gold in the snowboard superpipe in the Winter X Games and in the halfpipe at the Winter Olympics. In the Summer X Games, he was a silver medalist in skate vert. Then he made a triumphant return to the Dew Tour with a win in skate vert at the Wendy's Invitational in Portland in August.

Frequent Fliers

Robbie Maddison welcomed the new year in 2009 with a leap to the top of the replica Arc de Triomphe in Las Vegas. **Travis Pastrana** found his own extreme way to ring in 2010: On New Year's Eve, Pastrana drove his rally car off the pier in Long Beach, California. He landed, as planned, on a ramp that stood atop a barge floating in the harbor.

Pastrana's intent was to break the world record for a rally car jump (yes, someone really does keep track of such things!). Pastrana's 269-foot jump easily surpassed the old record of 171 feet set by **Ken Block** in 2006.

Not to be outdone, Maddison soared his motorcycle over the Corinth Canal in Greece in April of 2010. At the peak of his 279-foot jump from one side to the other, Maddison was 311 feet above the water below.

Skate Wars

Big money has come to professional skateboarding these days. Late in August, superstar **Rob Drydek**'s new Street League debuted in Phoenix. The Street Leaguers competed for the largest purse in skateboarding history—$1.2 million! That came on the heels of a $1 million

Snow to skate: Shaun White was a star in both!

Three in a row! Stephanie Gilmore came up from Australia to dominate women's surfing.

offer by Maloof Money Cup owners **Joe** and **Gavin Maloof**. The brothers—the Maloof family owns the NBA's Sacramento Kings—started the Maloof Money Cup in 2008 and awarded $100,000 to the winners of certain events. In the summer of 2009, the Maloofs offered a $1 million bonus to anyone who could win four Money Cups in a row. Only a week before the offer was made, **Chris Cole** had won his third in a row. But then Cole signed with Street League, which doesn't allow its skaters to participate in other competitions, so he couldn't go for the big prize after all!

Stay tuned . . . this could get interesting!

Surf's Up!

Australian **Stephanie Gilmore** has become the undisputed dominant force in women's surfing. In 2009, Gilmore won the Association of Surfing Professionals (ASP) women's world title for the third year in a row. She got off to a hot start in 2010, too, and was atop the standings in midsummer.

On the men's side, **Mick Fanning**, who's also from Australia, won his second world title in three years in 2009. American **Kelly Slater**, a nine-time ASP champion, fell to sixth place. In 2010, South African **Jordy Smith** made a run for his first title by taking over first place midway through the season.

Dew Tour

Jamie Bestwick was the Athlete of the Year on the Summer Dew Tour. Bestwick has won BMX vert five straight years.

On the Winter Dew Tour, California snowboarder **Jamie Anderson** was the women's Athlete of the Year. Norwegian skier **Andreas Hatveit** was the men's Athlete of the Year.

WINTER X GAMES

Gretchen Bleiler soared to a gold medal.

NEW KID ON THE BLOCK

Meet the Next Big Thing in extreme sports: **Bobby Brown**. He was the star of the 14th Winter X Games after taking home a pair of skiing gold medals in his rookie X Games performance. First, Brown won big air gold by pulling off a pair of brand-new tricks for a perfect score. The next night, Brown won the slopestyle competition to become the first skier to win two golds in a single Winter X Games.

LAVALLEE WINS BY KNOCK OUT

Snowmobile knock out was a new event at the Winter X Games, but the winner was a familiar one. It was **Levi LaVallee**, who earned the seventh X Games medal of his career.

If you don't know what knock out is, picture ski jumping—but on a snowmobile! Competitors build up speed down a long ramp and go airborne to post the longest jump possible. (Remember, kids, these are trained pros with proper safety equipment!) In each round, the competitor with the shortest jump is eliminated—or knocked out—until there is only one jumper left standing. LaVallee's winning jump measured 166 feet, 9 inches.

NEWS & NOTES

✳ Aspen resident **Gretchen Bleiler** bounced back from a fall in the 2009 X Games to win the women's snowboard superpipe in front of her hometown fans.

✳ **Tucker Hibbert** (snowmobile snocross) and **Nate Holland** (snowboarder X) dominated their events. Hibbert won by a whopping 28-second margin, while Holland won the gold medal for the fifth consecutive year.

✳ **Ophelie David** won the women's skier X for the fourth time in a row.

✳ **Shaun White** won the men's snowboard superpipe by pulling off a winning run in the final after a crash in the prelims that was so nasty, it knocked his helmet right off.

SUMMER X GAMES

Surprise Stunt

With a gold medal in the moto X freestyle competition already secured, **Travis Pastrana** only had to take a victory lap at the X Games in Los Angeles. But Pastrana doesn't do anything halfway. Instead of playing it safe, he went out and wowed the fans and his fellow competitors with a double backflip on his motocross bike. "That was just for the fans," Pastrana said. "It's the X Games—you've got to go big!"

Double the Fun

The rally car event has been a staple of the X Games, but this year an additional event made its debut: superrally. Instead of just two cars, each racing in their own lanes (as in rally, pictured here), superrally featured four cars competing on the same course. That made for a whole lot of bumping and banging as drivers jockeyed for position, especially on the turns.

American **Tanner Foust**, who competed in rallycross in Europe in 2010, won the gold medal in both rally and superrally. Fellow American **Brian Deegan** took the silver in both events.

News & Notes

➔ **Shaun White**'s silver medal in skate vert was impressive. But **Pierre-Luc Gagnon** won the gold for the third year in a row.

➔ **Ashley Fiolek** won the women's super X for the second year in a row. No need to talk about how Fiolek has overcome being deaf. We just have to say she's really, really good.

➔ **Cam Sinclair** won the moto X best trick event with a double backflip—the same trick that sent him into a life-threatening coma when he crashed during an X-Fighters competition in the summer of 2009.

➔ **Pedro Barros** won the skate park competition. At 15, Barros was younger than the 16-year-old X Games!

Antoine L'Estage flies over Kenny Brack during the rally car event.

2009-10 X GAMES WINNERS

Jen Hudak won her fourth X Games medal: her first gold.

WINTER X GAMES 14 • Aspen, Colorado
January 27–31, 2010

Skiing Big Air
Bobby Brown

Mono Skier X
Tyler Walker

Skier X (Men)
Chris Del Bosco

Skier X (Women)
Ophelie David

Skiing Slopestyle (Men)
Bobby Brown

Skiing Slopestyle (Women)
Kaya Turski

Skiing SuperPipe (Men)
Kevin Rolland

Skiing SuperPipe (Women)
Jen Hudak

Skiing SuperPipe High Air
Peter Olenick

Snowboard Big Air
Halldor Helgason

Snowboard Slopestyle (Men)
Eero Ettala

Snowboard Slopestyle (Women)
Jenny Jones

Snowboarder X (Men)
Nate Holland

Snowboarder X (Women)
Lindsey Jacobellis

Snowboard SuperPipe (Men)
Shaun White

Snowboard SuperPipe (Women)
Gretchen Bleiler

Snowmobile Best Trick
Heath Frisby

Snowmobile Freestyle
Justin Hoyer

Snowmobile Knock Out
Levi LaVallee

Snowmobile SnoCross
Tucker Hibbert

Snowmobile Adaptive SnoCross
Mike Schultz

SUMMER X GAMES 16 • Los Angeles, California
July 28–August 1, 2010

BMX Big Air
Chad Kagy

BMX Freestyle Street
Garrett Reynolds

BMX Freestyle Park
Daniel Dhers

BMX Freestyle Vert
Jamie Bestwick

Moto X Best Trick
Cam Sinclair

Moto X Best Whip
Todd Potter

Moto X Freestyle
Travis Pastrana

**Moto X
Speed & Style**
Travis Pastrana

Moto X Step Up
Matt Buyten

Moto X Super X (Men)
Josh Grant

Moto X Super X (Women)
Ashley Fiolek

Moto X Super X Adaptive
Mike Schultz

Rally Car Racing
Tanner Foust

Rally Car SuperRally
Tanner Foust

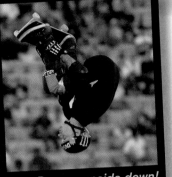

Jake Brown—upside down!

Skateboard Big Air
Jake Brown

Skateboard Big Air Rail Jam
Bob Burnquist

Game of SK8
Tommy Sandoval

Skateboard Street (Men)
Ryan Sheckler

Skateboard Street (Women)
Alexis Sablone

Skateboard Park
Pedro Barros

Skateboard Park Legends
Christian Hosol

Skateboard Vert (Men)
Pierre-Luc Gagnon

Skateboard Vert (Women)
Gaby Ponce

Skateboard Vert (Amateur)
Italo Penarrubia

Skateboard Vert Best Trick
Pierre-Luc Gagnon

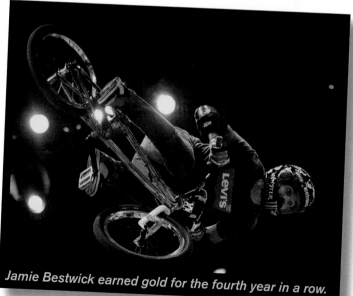

Jamie Bestwick earned gold for the fourth year in a row.

SOCCER

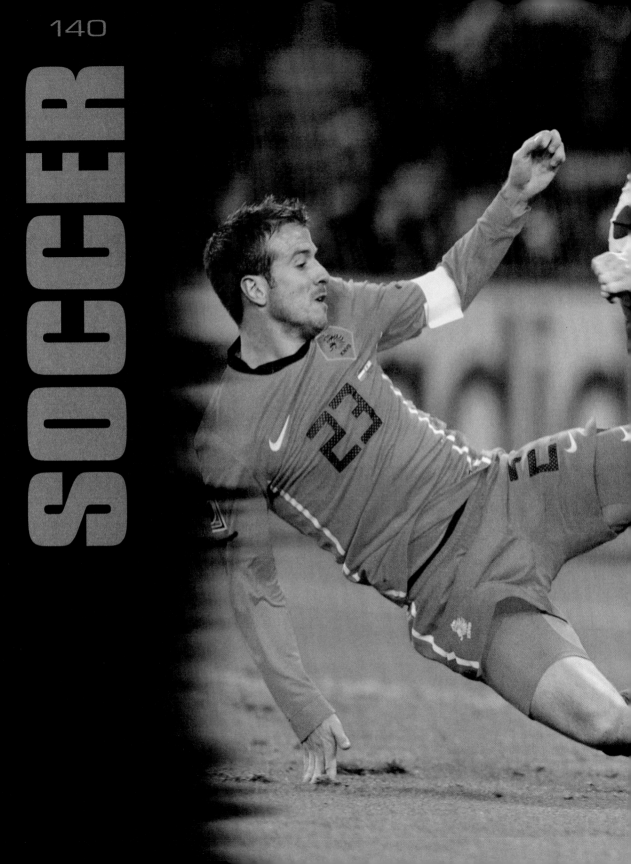

CUP-WINNING KICK!

Spain's Andres Iniesta smacked this shot past sliding Dutch defender Rafael van der Vaart and into the net for the only goal of the World Cup final. The goal gave Spain its first-ever World Cup and capped off a month of amazing soccer in South Africa. The Cup featured great goals, stunning mistakes, and enormous spirit. Plus, of course . . . the vuvuzelas!

WORLD CUP, ¡VIVA ESPAÑA!

For the first time ever, Spanish players hoisted the famous trophy.

The eyes of the world turned to South Africa for a month for the 2010 World Cup . . . and the players and fans put on quite a show. After 64 games, two teams emerged to stand on the ultimate sports stage. More than 700 million people tuned in to watch Spain beat the Netherlands, 1–0, in extra time to capture its first-ever World Cup championship.

The final was a real battle, with the referee handing out a record 14 yellow cards (and 1 red card). The Netherlands chose to try to outmuscle the Spanish offense, which relies on quick passes and ball control. Any Spaniard with the ball at his feet could count on a Dutch player trying to take him off his feet. This style of play lowered the number of quality shots, but both teams did have their chances. Dutch goalie **Maarten Stekenlenburg** saved a close-range header by **Sergio Ramos** in the 5th minute. Then, in the 62nd minute, Spanish goalie (and captain) **Iker Casillas** matched that with a stop of **Arjen Robben** on a breakaway. The game was tense and exciting, but after 90 minutes neither team had scored.

In the first 20 minutes of extra time, the score remained the same, but with just about 4 minutes to go, Spain brought the ball down the left wing. It was crossed over

THE FINAL 8

QUARTERFINALS

Netherlands 2, Brazil 1
Uruguay 1, Ghana 1 (4–2)
Germany 4, Argentina 0
Spain 1, Paraguay 0

SEMIFINALS

Spain 1, Germany 0
Netherlands 3, Uruguay 2

WORLD CUP FINAL

Spain 1, Netherlands 0

BRRRAAAPPPP!

What made the most noise at the World Cup? An opening day crowd that watched South Africa tie Mexico? Spanish fans after their Cup-winning goal? No, it was a three-foot piece of plastic called a vuvuzela. Thousands of soccer nuts blew the horns endlessly during every World Cup game. Fans in the stadiums said they suffered ringing in their ears for days. TV fans back home complained that the constant buzzing drowned out the announcers.

the top of the Dutch defense to a wide-open **Andres Iniesta**. The little midfielder didn't miss his chance, blasting a right-footed shot past Stekelenburg and into the far side of the net. The goal set off a celebration on the pitch, in the stadium, and throughout cities in Spain, which had waited so long for its chance at ultimate soccer glory. A few minutes later, it was over and Spain was the champion.

Here were some other memorable moments of the 2010 World Cup:

◎ **Swiss Shocker:** In the first round, tiny Switzerland shocked the eventual champ, upsetting Spain, 1–0.

◎ **German Power:** Germany scored four goals in wins over Australia, England, and Argentina.

◎ **Uruguay Surprise:** Not usually among the great South American sides, Uruguay made it all the way to the semifinals, sparked by superstar **Diego Forlan**.

◎ **Early Exits:** France imploded and was out in the first round. Italy didn't win and was out early, too. Brazil, to everyone's surprise, lost in the quarterfinals.

◎ **Ghana's Gaffe:** After Uruguay's **Luis Suarez** knocked a sure goal away with his hands, Ghana missed the penalty kick that would have ended the game and given Africa a team in the semifinals. Instead, Uruguay won the game on a penalty-kick shootout.

◎ **Power Shot:** In the Netherlands' 3–2 win over Uruguay, Dutch defender **Giovanni van Bronckhorst** unleashed the most amazing shot of the tournament. He blasted a 42-meter, left-footed shot into the upper right corner of the net.

Wham! Van Bronckhorst (in orange) unleashes a shot.

U.S. CUP REPORT

England 1, U.S. 1

Thank you, **Robert Green**! That's what U.S. fans were saying after the 1–1 tie with England in the first game of the Cup for both teams. After England scored in the fifth minute, Green, the English goalie, made one of the biggest goofs ever, letting a **Clint Dempsey** shot roll right past him after he'd stopped it. The tie gave the U.S. a big lift heading into the upcoming games.

Slovenia 2, U.S. 2

Uh-oh. Another early goal put the U.S. in a hole. It got worse when Slovenia scored again before halftime. But in a true show of sporting guts, the U.S. team rallied back. First, star **Landon Donovan** nearly took the Slovenian goalie's head off with a blistering shot. Then **Michael Bradley** knocked in a rebound to tie the score. A late "goal" by **Maurice Edu** was waved off by the referee, though no one was ever quite sure why! It was a great "win."

U.S. 1, Algeria 0

All the U.S. needed was a win over a team that had only barely qualified for the Cup and that was ranked 33rd in the world. The Americans took all the time they had and then some. Landon Donovan was again the hero, banging in a rebound (left) in the third minute of injury time, setting off celebrations in South Africa and around the U.S. The Americans were through to the second round!

Ghana 2, U.S. 1

After giving up yet another early penalty kick by Donovan. However, a score by **Asamoah Gyan** early in extra time ended the Americans' World Cup hopes . . . this time around.

WORLD CUP NOTES

England got robbed on this "nongoal" call.

REF GOOFS

The referees at the World Cup had an awful time. Their mistakes played a big part in way too many games.

* **Tevez was offside:** Against Mexico, Argentina star Carlos Tevez was so far offside when he scored, he was closer to the goal than ANY Mexican player!

* **The goal that wasn't:** Frank Lampard's long strike against Germany hit the crossbar and then bounced into the goal, but the ref said no. It would have tied the score, and England ended up losing, 4–1.

* **Edu who?:** The ref spotted a foul as U.S. halfback Maurice Edu scored what would have been a winning goal against Slovenia, but the alleged foul canceled the score.

* **Attack of Spain:** As Paraguay tried to take a penalty, four Spanish players charged in too early. The Paraguayan missed . . . but Spain wasn't caught.

In the final, English referee Howard Webb gave out an all-time record 14 yellow cards, plus 1 red card. Anyone with a whistle was probably glad when the World Cup finally ended.

THE GOLDEN BOOT AND BALL

The World Cup goes to a team, but there are individual awards. Uruguay's Diego Forlan scored beautiful goals and won the Golden Ball as the tournament's most outstanding player. Thomas Müller of Germany earned himself the Golden Boot after scoring five goals. Three other players also scored five times in the World Cup, but Müller's three assists broke the tie. Spanish goalie Iker Casillas had five shutouts, including the final, and won the Golden Glove as the top goalkeeper in the tournament.

Forlan was simply fabulous.

A "REAL" UPSET

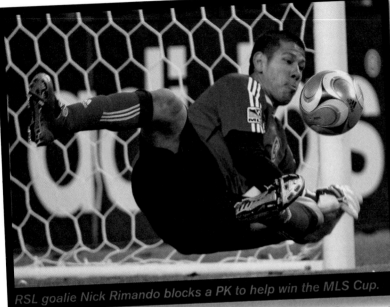

RSL goalie Nick Rimando blocks a PK to help win the MLS Cup.

Spanish club, Real Madrid, not "real" (reel) Salt Lake.) RSL had barely squeaked into the play-offs, qualifying as the eighth overall seed, nipping ninth-place Toronto and Colorado by just one win. However, they were tied for second in MLS in total goals scored, so there was hope.

That hope paid off when RSL went on an upset binge in the postseason. First they knocked off the Columbus Crew, who had the best regular-season record in MLS. Then they beat the Chicago Fire after a dramatic penalty-kick shootout.

In the MLS Cup itself, they took on the powerhouse Los Angeles Galaxy. RSL fell behind, 1–0, but a 64th-minute goal by striker **Robbie Findley** tied the game. In another PK shootout, RSL prevailed when stars **Landon Donovan** and **Edson**

C oming into the 2009 Major League Soccer play-offs, few fans outside of Utah thought that their team, Real Salt Lake, had much of a shot at the championship MLS Cup. (By the way, for those of you who are not soccer fans, that's pronounced "ray-AHL" Salt Lake, after the name of a famous

2009 MLS FINAL STANDINGS

EASTERN CONFERENCE	POINTS	WESTERN CONFERENCE	POINTS
Columbus Crew	49	L.A. Galaxy	48
Chicago Fire	45	Houston Dynamo	48
New England Revolution	42	Seattle Sounders FC	47
D.C. United	40	Chivas USA	45
Toronto FC	39	Real Salt Lake	40
Kansas City Wizards	33	Colorado Rapids	40
New York Red Bulls	21	FC Dallas	39

Champs! Real Salt Lake was real happy!

SuperLiga Results

For the third year, four top MLS clubs faced off against a quartet of big Mexican soccer teams in SuperLiga. The games were fiercely contested at stadiums throughout the U.S., with each group trying to uphold its national and league honor. The New England Revolution and Monarcas Morelia met in the final.

Buddle of the Galaxy missed their kicks. RSL's **Robbie Russell** didn't miss, and the team from Utah became the unlikely winner of the 14th MLS Cup.

The shootout miss was a rare low point for Buddle, who had had one his best seasons as a pro, scoring 5 goals for L.A. His performance helped him earn a spot on the U.S. World Cup team. For Donovan, it was a disappointing end to one of his best MLS seasons, as he won the league MVP for the second time by scoring 12 goals.

Other MLS Stars

The 2009 season included goals-scored leader **Jeff Cunningham** of FC Dallas, with 17, and top goalie **Zach Thornton** of the Chicago Fire, who allowed an average of only 0.87 goals per game, including 12 shutouts.

Women's Professional Soccer

On the women's side, WPS played its third season in 2010 and will expand to eight teams in 2011. Looking back on the 2009 season, New Jersey–based Sky Blue FC took the title, beating the Los Angeles Sol, 1–0, in the championship game.

Give Him a Hand!

Irish fans in the New York area have a new sports star to boo. French international star **Thierry Henry** joined the New York Red Bulls after the 2010 World Cup. Though a longtime star for his country and one of the top goal scorers in his prime, he earned Irish fans' anger during a World Cup qualifying match. Late in a 2009 game against Ireland, Henry knocked a ball down with his hand, then with his arm, and then scored. It was the only goal of the game. It gave France a trip to the World Cup and kept Ireland from going.

STAT STUFF

MAJOR LEAGUE SOCCER
CHAMPIONS

Year	Champion
2009	Real Salt Lake
2008	Columbus Crew
2007	Houston Dynamo
2006	Houston Dynamo
2005	Los Angeles Galaxy
2004	D.C. United
2003	San Jose Earthquakes
2002	Los Angeles Galaxy
2001	San Jose Earthquakes
2000	Kansas City Wizards
1999	D.C. United
1998	Chicago Fire
1997	D.C. United
1996	D.C. United

World Cup Scoring Leaders

MEN
GOALS	PLAYER, COUNTRY
15	Ronaldo, Brazil
14	Miroslav Klose, Germany
14	Gerd Müller, West Germany
13	Just Fontaine, France
12	Pelé, Brazil
11	Jürgen Klinsmann, Germany
11	Sandor Kocsis, Hungary

WOMEN
GOALS	PLAYER, COUNTRY
14	Birgit Prinz, Germany
12	Michelle Akers, United States
11	Sun Wen, China
11	Bettina Wiegmann, Germany

WORLD CUP RESULTS

YEAR	WINNER	RUNNER-UP
2010	**Spain**	Netherlands
2006	**Italy**	France
2002	**Brazil**	Germany
1998	**France**	Brazil
1994	**Brazil**	Italy
1990	**West Germany**	Argentina
1986	**Argentina**	West Germany
1982	**Italy**	West Germany
1978	**Argentina**	Netherlands
1974	**West Germany**	Netherlands
1970	**Brazil**	Italy
1966	**England**	West Germany
1962	**Brazil**	Czechoslovakia
1958	**Brazil**	Sweden
1954	**West Germany**	Hungary
1950	**Uruguay**	Brazil
1938	**Italy**	Hungary
1934	**Italy**	Czechoslovakia
1930	**Uruguay**	Argentina

Note: The World Cup was canceled in 1942 and 1946 due to World War II.

GOLF'S UPS AND DOWNS

Tiger Woods once again dominated the world of golf in the past year. For the first part of the year, it was for his amazing play on the course. After recovering from knee surgery in early 2009, he ended the golf year winning the FedEx Cup (and a tidy $10 million!). He earned the final points he needed for that big prize by finishing second in the season-ending Tour Championship to **Phil Mickelson**.

For his part, Mickelson had missed a lot of 2009 caring for his wife, who was battling cancer. He still earned enough points to finish second in the FedEx Cup race.

As 2010 began, both those golfers

2009
MAJOR CHAMPIONSHIP WINNERS

THE MASTERS
Phil Mickelson

THE U.S. OPEN
Graeme McDowell

THE BRITISH OPEN
Louis Oosthuizen

THE PGA CHAMPIONSHIP
Martin Kaymer

would be making headlines again, but for very different reasons. Woods had to leave golf for a while to deal with some personal issues. Without Woods, interest in golf dipped a bit. However, by the time of the Masters, the other name in the headlines took over. Phil Mickelson won his third Masters in Augusta, Georgia, in April. Mickelson became the face of golf.

The other 2010 majors went to lesser-known golfers from outside the United States. **Graeme McDowell** of Northern Ireland started the trend at the U.S. Open when he became the first European winner since 1970. He took advantage of a last-round collapse by American golfer **Dustin Johnson**, who would make more news later in the summer.

First, though, at the British Open in July, an unknown South African named **Louis Oosthuizen** won by an amazing seven strokes! It was the biggest win in the fabled tournament since Woods's triumph in 2000.

The trend continued at the PGA Championship. German golfer **Martin Kaymer** surprised everyone by hanging on to win a play-off. However, he didn't have to face Dustin Johnson. In a shocking turnaround, Johnson was penalized two strokes for touching his club in a bunker. He said that he didn't even know it was a bunker, but rules are rules. He went from tied for first to fifth place.

These winners and others were part of the other big story in golf for the past year: the continuing emergence of a crop of great young golfers (see page 155).

GOLF

"FORE" FOR PHIL!

Lefty Phil Mickelson helped his wife battle cancer and then he battled the world's most famous golf course, winning the Masters in Georgia in April. It was the third green jacket (given to the Masters winner) and fourth major for Mickelson.

2009 PRESIDENTS CUP

Woods got five big points for the U.S. team.

The two big international team golf events are the Ryder Cup and the Presidents Cup. The Ryder Cup was held in October 2010, too late to include in our book, but the 2009 Presidents Cup gave U.S. fans a reason to celebrate.

Held every four years, the Presidents Cup pits a team of American golfers against a field of international players who are not from Europe (since that's what the Ryder Cup is about). At Harding Park in San Francisco in October 2009, the U.S. team whipped the Internationals by five points.

Tiger Woods was a key star for the U.S. team. He teamed with world No. 3 **Steve Stricker** to form a dominant pair in the early rounds (the Presidents Cup uses several formats of team golf, including best-ball and foursomes). On the final day of singles match play, Woods's victory over **Y. E. Yang** (who had beaten him earlier at the 2009 PGA Championship) clinched the Cup for America. He became the third player ever with a perfect 5–0 record in the Cup.

A BIG PAIN IN THE NECK

At the Players Championship in May, something else weird happened to golfing great **Tiger Woods**: He had to stop playing in the middle of a round. In fact, it was the final round, and he was two under for the tournament. He wasn't near the lead; **Tim Clark** ended up winning the event. Woods was playing well when he hit his drive on the seventh hole and then bailed out. He had a neck injury and swinging the club was just too painful. He was out for several weeks—another blow for Woods in a tough year.

CHIP SHOTS

What a Finish!

When young Irish golfer **Rory McIlroy** (below) nearly missed the cut at the Quail Hollow Championship in North Carolina, it was actually the start of something big. In the next two rounds, he turned from barely in to top of the world. In the third round, he shot a 66 and then topped that with a course-record 62 to win it. At 20 years and 10 months, he became the youngest golfer since **Tiger Woods** to win a PGA tournament.

Like Father, Like Son

Bill Haas won the Bob Hope Classic in La Quinta, California, in January 2010. He hung on for a one-shot victory in the 90-hole event. Bill's father, **Jay**, is also a pro golfer and won the same tournament in 1988! "It's definitely neat that down the road, 22 years from now, we can look at both our names on the list here," Bill Haas said. Later in the year, they became the first father-son pair to qualify for the Players Championship!

59 + 60 = Amazing

For only the fourth time in PGA history, a golfer shot a 59 in an official round. **Paul Goydos** accomplished the feat in the first round of the John Deere Classic in Illinois. But that's not all—on the same day at the same tournament, **Steve Stricker** shot a 60! Their low score combo marked the first time those two scores were shot on the same day. Stricker got the last laugh, however, going on to win the tournament over Goydos by two strokes. The low-scoring binge continued that summer, as yet another golfer accomplished the feat. **Stuart Appleby** shot a 59 on the final round of the Greenbrier Classic to win the event.

Who's Next?

With Phil Mickelson and Tiger Woods battling age and injury, it's time for some new, young golfers to charge to the front of the pack. Here are some names to watch in the coming years:

RICKIE FOWLER: He had earned more than $2.5 million in his rookie season through only July.

RYO ISHIKAWA: In May, on the same day that McIlroy shot his 62 (see left), Ishikawa became the first golfer to record a 58 on a major pro circuit, carding that amazing number in a Japan Tour event.

DUSTIN JOHNSON: He has the game to bounce back from two tough losses in 2010 majors.

▲ **RORY MCILROY:** His 62 at Quail Hollow (see above) and a stunning first-round 63 at the British Open were the latest big moments in his young career.

LPGA NEWS

She's No. 1! ▶▶▶

With the retirement of **Lorena Ochoa** (see box below), the spot at the top of the World Golf Rankings opened up for the first time since 2007. Since the rankings were started in 2004, no American woman had enjoyed time at the top. **Cristie Kerr** changed all that in June 2010 with a dominating win at the LPGA Championship. She whomped the field, winning by an all-time record 12 strokes! She led from the start and was well under par in all four rounds. It was her second major championship (she won the U.S. Women's Open in 2007), and the points she earned vaulted her to the top of the world rankings.

¡ADIOS, LORENA!

Last year in this space, we waved so long to **Annika Sorenstam**. This year, another all-time golfing legend says *adiós*. Mexican golfer **Lorena Ochoa** won three straight Player of the Year awards (2007–2009), two majors, and 27 tournaments (and $15 million) in her short career. Still only 28 and ranked No. 1 in the world, she is leaving the game to start a family with her husband, Andres Conesa. With her departure, the LPGA has lost a great player and perhaps its most famous face.

◄◄◄ Finally!

For almost a decade, **Michelle Wie** has been the "next big thing" in women's golf. As a teenager, she was playing with the pro ladies and even played in some men's tournaments. Her talent was obvious, but she never quite lived up to all the hype. In November 2009, however, she won an LPGA tournament, the Lorena Ochoa Invitational, played in Guadalajara, Mexico. Still only 20 and a full-time student at Stanford, Wie might finally be emerging into the greatness so long predicted for her.

Far East Power ▶▶▶

The success of golfers from Asian countries continued in the LPGA in 2009 and 2010. Korea boasted 33 golfers ranked in the top 100 in the world. One Korean golfer, **Jiyai Shin**, was the LPGA's 2009 earnings leader. Japan's **Ai Miyazato** (right) was the leader on the money list through the middle of 2010. Through July 2010, **Cristie Kerr** was the only non-Asian-based golfer to win an LPGA tournament, with Miyazato's four wins topping the charts.

Pink Paula

Talented **Paula Creamer** overcame an injured thumb to earn her first major tournament victory at the 2010 U.S. Women's Open at the famed Oakmont Country Club in Pennsylvania. Wearing her traditional pink outfit, Creamer led from the start and won by four shots.

THE MAJORS

In golf, some tournaments are known as the majors. They're the four most important events of the year on either the men's or women's pro tours. Tiger Woods is rapidly moving up the ranks in career wins in majors. On the women's side, Annika Sorenstam has the most among recent golfers.

MEN'S

GOLFER	MASTERS	U.S. OPEN	BRITISH OPEN	PGA CHAMP.	TOTAL
Jack **NICKLAUS**	6	4	3	5	18
Tiger **WOODS**	4	3	3	4	14
Walter **HAGEN**	0	2	4	5	11
Ben **HOGAN**	2	4	1	2	9
Gary **PLAYER**	3	1	3	2	9
Tom **WATSON**	2	1	5	0	8
Arnold **PALMER**	4	1	2	0	7
Gene **SARAZEN**	1	2	1	3	7
Sam **SNEAD**	3	0	1	3	7
Harry **VARDON**	0	1	6	0	7

WALTER HAGEN

In golf's early days, it was not considered "gentlemanly" to play the game as a pro, that is, to make money at it. Walter Hagen changed all that. By bringing his amazing skills to the game and boldly striking out as the first touring pro, Hagen set the stage for what golf has become today: an international, big-money sport. Hagen won 11 major championships (third-most all-time) in his career, which took place mostly in the years between the world wars. Without Hagen, there might be no **Tiger Woods**.

WOMEN'S

GOLFER	LPGA	USO	BO	NAB	MAUR	TH	WES	TOTAL
Patty **BERG**	0	1	x	x	x	7	7	15
Mickey **WRIGHT**	4	4	x	x	x	2	3	13
Louise **SUGGS**	1	2	x	x	x	4	4	11
Annika **SORENSTAM**	3	3	1	3	x	x	x	10
Babe **ZAHARIAS**	x	3	x	x	x	3	4	10
Betsy **RAWLS**	2	4	x	x	x	x	2	8
Juli **INKSTER**	2	2	x	2	1	x	x	7
Karrie **WEBB**	1	2	1	2	1	x	x	7

KEY: LPGA = LPGA Championship, USO = U.S. Open, BO = British Open, NAB = Nabisco Championship, MAUR = Du Maurier (1979–2000), TH = Titleholders (1937–1972), WES = Western Open (1937–1967)

PGA TOUR CAREER EARNINGS*

1	Tiger Woods	$93,587,538
2	Vijay Singh	$62,914,865
3	Phil Mickelson	$59,055,494
4	Jim Furyk	$45,640,256
5	Davis Love III	$39,968,818
6	Ernie Els	$39,751,585
7	David Toms	$32,334,447
8	Kenny Perry	$31,514,332
9	Justin Leonard	$29,799,148
10	Stewart Cink	$28,902,977

LPGA TOUR CAREER EARNINGS*

1	Annika Sorenstam	$22,573,192
2	Karrie Webb	$15,669,992
3	Lorena Ochoa	$14,862,664
4	Juli Inkster	$12,836,081
5	Cristie Kerr	$11,424,856

*Through July 2010

Babe Zaharias

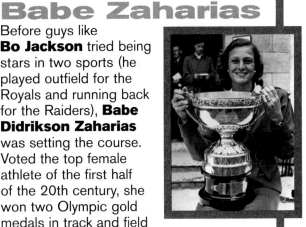

Before guys like **Bo Jackson** tried being stars in two sports (he played outfield for the Royals and running back for the Raiders), **Babe Didrikson Zaharias** was setting the course. Voted the top female athlete of the first half of the 20th century, she won two Olympic gold medals in track and field and played many different sports. Perhaps her greatest success came in golf, in which she won 55 tournaments, including three U.S. Opens, in a career cut short by cancer in 1956. One of the founders of the LPGA in 1949, she is still ranked as one of the best all-around athletes ever, male or female.

TENNIS

ROCKIN' RAFFY!
Spanish powerhouse Rafael Nadal moved to the top of the world rankings in 2010. How long can he stay on top?

NADAL ON THE RISE!

The biggest story in tennis for the past four years has been the phenomenal rise of Swiss star Roger Federer. He became the all-time leader in Grand Slam championships, and some experts call him the best player of all time. However, in 2010, cracks started to appear in his dominant game. First, Federer lost the final at the 2009 U.S. Open to unheralded Juan Martin del Potro. Federer did win the Australian Open in early 2010 for his record 16th Grand Slam title, but then his success slowed.

Spanish lefty Rafael Nadal staked his claim as the new "best in the world" by winning the French Open. Following his championship at Roland Garros, Nadal moved into first place in the world rankings. Federer soon fell all the way to No. 3, behind No. 2 Novak Djokovic. It was the lowest that Federer had ranked since November 2003.

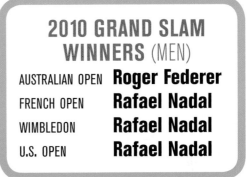

2010 GRAND SLAM WINNERS (MEN)

AUSTRALIAN OPEN	**Roger Federer**
FRENCH OPEN	**Rafael Nadal**
WIMBLEDON	**Rafael Nadal**
U.S. OPEN	**Rafael Nadal**

Once just a clay court specialist, Nadal continued to shine in 2010, adding a victory at Wimbledon, a tournament in which Federer saw his streak of 23 straight Grand Slam semifinal berths end.

Among U.S. male players, Andy Roddick remained the highest ranked, but he dropped to No. 9 by midyear after some disappointing results in big tournaments.

A LOOOOONG MATCH

During a Wimbledon tennis match, a marathon broke out. American John Isner (below left) and French player Nicolas Mahut amazed the sports world by playing a match that lasted 11 hours, 5 minutes. They took an all-time record 138 games to complete the final set! At Wimbledon, you have to win the fifth set by two games. The players swapped wins in games past 5–5. The fifth set took eight hours, 11 minutes, before Isner won, 70–68!

The match started on a Tuesday and ended on a Thursday; it was broken into three very long sections due to darkness. Isner also set a record with 112 aces, much more than the old single-match record of 78. "It stinks that someone had to lose," Isner said afterward.

MORE OF THE SAME

That's what women's tennis fans enjoyed in late 2009 and most of 2010. Serena Williams continued to dominate, winning two more Grand Slam tournaments. She was also dubbed "the greatest of all time" by none other than *Sports Illustrated*.

It's hard to argue with that title, as she has won all four of the Grand Slam events and has more Slam victories than any player since Steffi Graf (see page 163).

She's not alone in the Williams family, of course. Sister Venus was second on the 2010 money list in women's pro tennis and was ranked third in the world. Though Venus has not won a Grand Slam event since Wimbledon in 2008, she has won four other tournaments in the past two seasons, along with a ton of money. (Venus also recorded the fastest serve of the year. One of her blasts at the French Open was recorded at 128 mph / 207 kph!) Together, the hard-hitting Williams sisters have rewritten the tennis record books and show no signs of slowing their march through history anytime soon.

Serena Williams is No. 1, but Eastern Europe is emerging as a world tennis hotbed. Russian Vera Zvonareva made it to the Wimbledon final before meeting the Serena Slam. Petra Kvitova of the Czech Republic made the semifinals, and Russia's Tsvetana Pironkova has beaten Venus Williams at two Grand Slam events. Bulgarian Yaroslava Shvedova teamed with American Vania King to win the Wimbledon doubles title in 2010. And Russian Dinara Safina was No. 1 in the world in 2009. Five of the top 25 women in the world (through July 2010) were Russian.

Serena leaps for joy after winning in Australia.

NICE CROWD!

It was only an exhibition, but it set a world record. A total of 35,681 people packed a stadium in Brussels, Belgium, beating the old record of 30,472, set way back in 1973. **Kim Clijsters** (right) of Belgium defeated **Serena Williams** in two sets. Fans got a bonus when **Martina Navratilova** (below), one of the greatest tennis legends of all time, served as the umpire for the match.

One thing that is changing is the age of players. For a while in the 1980s and 1990s, many of the world's top female tennis players were teenagers. **Tracy Austin**, **Jennifer Capriati**, and **Andrea Jaeger** were three of the biggest-name teen stars. However, by mid-July 2010, no teens were ranked in the top 30 worldwide. Only seven were in the top 100.

Another big story was the rise of **Kim Clijsters**, returning to tennis after a long break to land as high as No. 4 in the world.

2010 GRAND SLAM WINNERS (WOMEN)

AUSTRALIAN OPEN	**Serena Williams**
FRENCH OPEN	**Francesca Schiavone**
WIMBLEDON	**Serena Williams**
U.S. OPEN	**Kim Clijsters**

Martina's Big Battle

Tennis great **Martina Navratilova** won 59 Grand Slam singles, doubles, and mixed doubles events in her amazing career. She's been a great mentor to younger players and a positive force in tennis for decades. In April, the tennis world rallied to support her when she was diagnosed with breast cancer. After completing treatment, she returned to the court to great cheers when she took part in an invitational event at Wimbledon. Another victory for a tennis hero!

STAT STUFF

ALL-TIME GRAND SLAM CHAMPIONSHIPS (MEN)

	AUS. OPEN	FRENCH OPEN	WIMBLEDON	U.S. OPEN	TOTAL
Roger **FEDERER**	4	1	6	5	**16**
Pete **SAMPRAS**	2	0	7	5	**14**
Roy **EMERSON**	6	2	2	2	**12**
Björn **BORG**	0	6	5	0	**11**
Rod **LAVER**	3	2	4	2	**11**
Bill **TILDEN**	0	0	3	7	**10**
Jimmy **CONNORS**	1	0	2	5	**8**
Ivan **LENDL**	2	3	0	3	**8**
Fred **PERRY**	1	1	3	3	**8**
Ken **ROSEWALL**	4	2	0	2	**8**
Andre **AGASSI**	4	1	1	2	**8**
Rafael **NADAL**	1	5	2	0	**8**

BJORN BORG

The Swedish sensation had a short career, but he made the most of it. Borg started early, as the then-youngest winner of the French Open. He was just 17 when he won at Roland Garros, where he would end up with six titles. He also won five straight Wimbledon championships, starting when he was 18 in 1976. Borg also helped Sweden capture its first Davis Cup in 1975, and he would end his career with a record 33 straight Davis Cup singles wins. He retired at 26, his legend assured.

ALL-TIME GRAND SLAM CHAMPIONSHIPS (WOMEN)

	AUS.	FRENCH	WIMBLEDON	U.S.	TOTAL
Margaret Smith **COURT**	11	5	3	5	**24**
Steffi **GRAF**	4	6	7	5	**22**
Helen Wills **MOODY**	0	4	8	7	**19**
Chris **EVERT**	2	7	3	6	**18**
Martina **NAVRATILOVA**	3	2	9	4	**18**
Serena **WILLIAMS**	5	1	4	3	**13**
Billie Jean **KING**	1	1	6	4	**12**
Maureen **CONNOLLY**	1	2	3	3	**9**
Monica **SELES**	4	3	0	2	**9**
Suzanne **LENGLEN**	0	2*	6	0	**8**
Molla Bjurstedt **MALLORY**	0	0	0	8	**8**

*Also won four French titles before 1925; in those years, the tournament was open only to French nationals.

STEFFI GRAF

Combining power and determination, **Steffi Graf** dominated tennis during her career. Her 22 Grand Slam titles are second-most all-time. Through the late 1980s and the entire 1990s, Graf won more than 100 pro tournaments, including 7 Wimbledons. Her greatest year was 1988, when she became the third woman to win all four Grand Slam tournaments in one year (after **Maureen Connolly** in 1959 and **Margaret Smith Court** in 1970). Graf's strength was legendary, but her competitiveness was what set her above her peers.

OTHER SPORTS

PARIS BY PEDAL!

At the 2010 Tour de France, Spain's Alberto Contador captured his third victory in the last four runnings (pedalings?) of this famous race. He's in the race leader's yellow jersey as the field cycles down the Champs-Elysées in Paris with the famed Arc de Triomphe in the background. Read more about Contador and other "other" sportspeople inside!

BEACH VOLLEYBALL

After the 2009 pro beach volleyball season ended, the team on top was no surprise. Coming off their amazing 2008 season, in which they won an Olympic gold medal, **Todd Rogers** and **Phil Dalhausser** were on a mighty roll. They won eight events in 2009, and the Association of Volleyball Professionals (AVP) title.

The first half of 2010 was no different. They won four of the first five events and had nine wins on the World Tour events. The nine wins in the World Tour gave them an all-time record for one season—topping the old record of four set in 2008 by, well . . . guess who? That's

right: Rogers and Dalhausser. It's a good thing that beach volleyball players don't need much gear; packing light eased the duo's long trips to places like Brazil, Italy, and Russia.

The women's AVP tour was getting a bit more competitive, as **Kerri Walsh** took time off to have a baby. Her longtime playing partner, **Misty May-Treanor**, the winningest woman ever on the beach, teamed with another veteran, **Nicole Branagh**. They were pushed by **Jennifer Kessy** and **April Ross**, whose three wins put them atop the standings in midsummer. However, on August 13, 2010, bad news hit the entire AVP Tour.

All events after that date were canceled when the organizers of the Tour ran out of money. The AVP has always struggled to stay in business. This latest blow will be hard to come back from. Beach volleyball fans are crossing their fingers that the Tour will come back in 2011.

Dalhausser and Rogers continued their dominance in beach volleyball.

TRACK AND FIELD

With no world championships in track and field this year (they're held every other year), U.S. attention focused on the 2010 national championships in late June.

★ One of the biggest stories was that of **Lolo Jones**. The 100-meter hurdles specialist had Olympic gold in her grasp in 2008, but she fell over the final hurdle. This summer, she won the national championship. It's another step toward her goal of returning to the Olympics and coming back a winner.

★ In the 100-meter sprint, **Allyson Felix** was the winner. She hopes the title will be a springboard to gold, which she also just missed in Beijing in 2008.

★ **Chaunte Lowe** broke a national record in the high jump, soaring 6 feet, 8 ¾ inches. She must like leaping: Lowe also finished second in the long jump!

★ Another record fell when **Kara Patterson**'s javelin landed in the grass. She hurled the spear 218 feet, 9 inches to take home the national title.

Lolo Jones breaks the tape and wins!

★ In the all-around events, **Hyleas Fountain** won her fourth national heptathlon title, while **Jake Arnold** held off former champ **Tom Pappas** to win the decathlon.

What Did Bolt Do?

The world's fastest human, **Usain Bolt** of Jamaica, did not have as many big stages in 2010, but he made the most of the ones he did have. He posted the year's best time in the 200 and even raced in the rarely run 300-meter race. He also had the fastest time of the year in the 100 meters at 9.82 (a time that was later matched by **Asafa Powell**). However, at a 100-meter race in Sweden in August, Bolt was beaten by American **Tyson Gay**. Track fans were shocked. It was Bolt's first loss in almost three years. Saying he wanted to rest, Bolt took the rest of the year off to look ahead to the 2012 Olympics.

RACING

Jumpin' Jockeys!

In horse racing, it's usually the animals who are the stars. They're the "athletes," battling nose-to-nose to make it to the finish line first. However, in 2010, the Triple Crown helped elevate one of the jockeys into the spotlight. **Calvin Borel** did something no jockey had ever done in the 136-year history of the famed Kentucky Derby: By leading **Super Saver** to victory in May, Borel won his third Derby in the past four years. (He also won on **Mine That Bird** in 2009 and on **Street Sense** in 2007.)

Super Saver (right) steams ahead.

However, Borel and Super Saver couldn't repeat in the Preakness, which was won by **Lookin' at Lucky**, so another year went by without a new Triple Crown champion (when one horse wins all three key races). This stretch since 1978, when **Affirmed** won it, is the longest ever without a Triple Crown winner.

In the Belmont Stakes, the third leg of the Triple Crown, another jockey got a milestone win. After losing 11 previous Belmonts, veteran **Mike Smith** guided **Drosselmeyer** to victory. It also gave trainer **Bill Mott** his first Belmont Stakes win.

Borel counts his Derby victories.

2009 Triple Crown Winners

RACE	TRACK	HORSE	JOCKEY
KENTUCKY DERBY	Churchill Downs	Super Saver	Calvin Borel
PREAKNESS	Pimlico	Lookin' at Lucky	Martin Garcia
BELMONT STAKES	Belmont Park	Drosselmeyer	Mike Smith

Three for Alberto! ▶▶▶

The 2010 Tour de France ended the same way as the 2009 race. **Alberto Contador** of Spain was the winner, followed closely by his new rival, **Andy Schleck** of Luxembourg. Contador took the lead for good a few days before the final ride, passing Schleck after Schleck's bike chain broke. Contador held on to capture his third Tour de France victory in the past four years.

The end of the 2010 race also saw the end of one of the most remarkable careers in American sports. **Lance Armstrong** finished nearly 40 minutes behind Contador. Armstrong said it was his last Tour de France, but he'll always be a huge part of its history. The amazing racer from Texas won seven of the historic races, two more than any other rider ever. His courage in coming back after beating cancer just made his legend even greater.

MUSH TO THE RECORD

In the famous Iditarod sled-dog race, **Lance Mackey** became the first driver (or musher, as they're known) to win four straight championships. Mackey and his 14 hardworking dogs took just under nine days to cover the grueling 1,150-mile course across Alaska's wilderness. Mackey's time missed the all-time fastest mark, set by **Martin Buser** in 2002, by just a few hours. The 2010 race also saw the end of one of the great careers in the event, as four-time winner **Jeff King** called it quits after 21 years of racing.

LACROSSE

U.S.A.: World lacrosse champs!

The U.S. men's team captured the World Lacrosse Championships played in England in July 2010. They knocked off Canada in the final. The victory avenged a loss to Canada in the 2006 world championships.

The Americans' 12–10 victory came after a week of fierce competition among 29 countries. There were supposed to be 30 countries, but a last-minute problem kept one of them from reaching England. And therein lies a story.

The sport of lacrosse was created by Native North Americans nearly 1,000 years ago. By the late 1800s, it had become a hugely popular sport in Canada. One native nation, the Iroquois, regarded lacrosse as a key part of their culture. Since 1980, the Iroquois have been recognized as a nation by international lacrosse, and their teams have finished fourth in the past three world championships. Not bad for a nation that has only about 125,000 people.

However, even though the U.S. made a special exception for the Iroquois team to travel to this year's event using Iroquois passports, England would not let the team enter with them. On principle, the team refused to travel with U.S. passports . . . and they stayed home. The uproar got the team more press than if they'd actually played, but the sadness of missing out remained. Expect them to be back for the next world championships in 2014.

National Lacrosse League
2010 Champs
Washington Stealth

Major League Lacrosse
2010 Champs
Chesapeake Bayhawks

Lewis Ratcliff of the Stealth

GYMNASTICS

There was good news for U.S. gymnastics at the World Championships in London in late 2009. **Bridget Sloan**, the reigning U.S. champ, took home gold from the worlds. She nipped her teammate **Rebecca Bross** for the title. They were not the only Americans to come home with medals: **Kayla Williams** won the vault event and **Ivana Hong** was third in the balance beam.

On the men's side, **Tim McNeill** was the highest U.S. finisher at seventh. **Kohei Uchimura** of Japan was the all-around champion. **Danell Leyva**'s fourth-place in the horizontal bar was the highest finish by a U.S. man in the various events.

Bridget Sloan

RODEO

Ridin', ropin', and steer wrasslin'. That's rodeo, y'all! The best cowboys in the world participate in the Professional Rodeo Cowboys Association tour. For most of the 2000s, they've all been chasing one guy: **Trevor Brazile** from, naturally, Texas. Brazile won again in 2009, giving him seven of the past eight all-around "top cowboy" titles. Brazile comes from a rodeo family: Both his mom and his dad were top rodeo performers. Brazile's best event is the tie-down, and he's good enough in all the others to be America's top cowboy again.

Brazile hops off to tie the calf.

The other big rodeo competition is on the Professional Bull Riders (PBR) tour. **Kody Lostroh** has been riding bulls since he was seven years old. The Colorado native started out young, but, he says, "I wasn't scared at all. It was the most fun thing I'd ever done and I wanted to keep doing it!" Good thing he did. In 2009, he reached the top, winning five events and piling up enough points to earn his first world PBR championship.

BOWLING

Kelly Kulick shows off her winning form.

often sees differences of only a few pins, Kulick beat **Chris Barnes** in the final match by 70 pins! Kulick got a ton of attention and articles in newspapers and magazines all over.

As for the rest of the bowling season, it was more of the same from a veteran. **Walter Ray Williams Jr.** led the PBA in earnings and points. He also became the oldest person, at 50, to win the Player of the Year (POY) award. He won the first of his seven POY awards way back in 1986! Williams also won his seventh ESPY Award from ESPN as the top U.S. bowler.

In July, **Stephen Shanabrook** probably wore out his bowling shoes. The man from Plano, Texas, set what is believed to be a world record by bowling for five days and five hours straight.

When bowling's Tournament of Champions began, **Kelly Kulick** was an asterisk. She had earned a special spot in the all-men's event as the women's world champion for 2009. By the end of the event in January 2010, what she had done was called by one writer "the greatest moment in women's sports."

What did she do? She won! Kulick became the first woman to win an all-men's event in the Professional Bowlers Association (PBA). It was not a squeaker of a win, either. In a sport that

2009–10
PBA Points Leaders

Walter Ray **WILLIAMS** Jr.	229,124
Bill **O'NEILL**	208,234
Mike **SCROGGINS**	195,259
Chris **BARNES**	192,492
Wes **MALOTT**	185,192

BOXING

The Ring in 2010

Boxing brothers Wladimir and Vitali

The biggest news in boxing was the fight that didn't happen. For a while, fight fans were excited about a possible battle between Filipino slugger **Manny Pacquiao** and American star **Floyd Mayweather Jr**. They are widely considered to be the two best boxers in the world. The two boxers' agents went back and forth for months, coming closer to a fight in Dallas's huge Cowboys Stadium. In the end, however, they could not agree. Pacquiao did fight **Joshua Clottey** in Dallas, while Mayweather whomped **Sugar Shane Mosley**. But those were not the fights fans wanted, and the wait continues for yet another Fight of the Century.

The other fight that fans would like to see also probably won't happen. The top two heavyweights in the world are brothers! **Wladimir Klitschko** is number one, while his brother **Vitali** is ranked second. Both won fights in 2010, but since they won't box against each other, the question of who would win in the Klitschko house will remain a mystery.

CHESS BOXING?

Play some chess. Box. Then play some more chess. Then box. Whoever gets checkmated or knocked out first is the loser. Now, that is a weird sport. Thanks to a book by famous sportswriter **Rick Reilly**, this obscure version of boxing got a lot of attention in 2010. Top chess boxers were featured on websites and in magazines, while the world chess boxing organization got bigger.

The sport is most often seen in Europe, and the best player-fighters are based there. There are weight classes, as in regular boxing. **Leo "Granit" Kraft** is the heavyweight champion. He's from Belarus but fights representing his home in Germany.

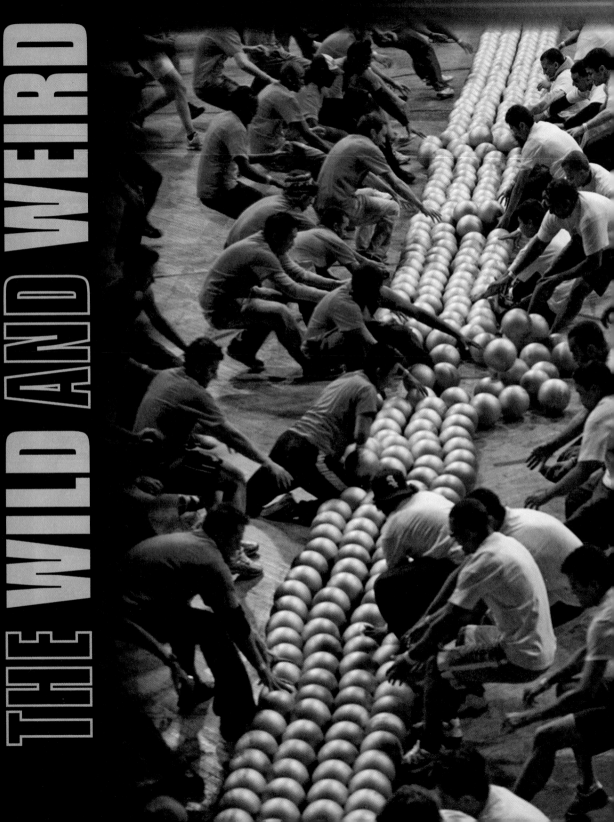

THE WILD AND WEIRD

Our book includes the greatest heroes in the sports world, the most important and most memorable moments of the sports year . . . and then there are these guys. Some people do sports just 'cause they love to do them . . . even if they're a bit offbeat.

◀Dodge This!

Dodgeball is a classic playground game of flinging squishy, bouncy balls at one another. Get hit, you're out. Catch the ball, the other guy's out. Easy, right? Now trying playing it with your entire school at once! On May 21, 2010, 712 people got together in New York City and set a new official world record for the largest dodgeball game ever. (Other larger groups claim they were biggest, but the world record people said they didn't follow all the rules . . . um, okay.) The teams of people in yellow and blue T-shirts fired silver rubber balls back and forth for half an hour until one team remained.

For those of you with way, way too much room in your brains: The blue team won this enormous game.

And It Stinks, Too! ▶

A bog is a big pile of goo. Really. It's like a swamp, but gooier. Bogs are wetlands, but they are firm enough in most places that you can walk on them. They're full of weeds, reeds, bugs, slugs, and swimmers.

Swimmers? Well, not really swimmers but snorkelers. The annual World Bog Snorkelling Championship is held every year at a stinky, gooey place in Wales called Waen Rhydd. Believe it or not, that is pronounced "wine reeth." Contestants plunge into a narrow channel dug into the bog. They have to snorkel the length of this brownish, greenish, slimy water. Fastest one wins! In 2009, winner **Conor Murphy** covered the 60-yard (55 m) course in 1 minute, 42 seconds. There's also a Bog Mountain Bike Championship.

at Dodger Stadium were led by rocker **Ozzy Osbourne** in setting a record for the loudest and longest scream! They screamed for nearly a minute at decibel levels above that of a jet! The event got a place in the *Guinness World Records* and helped raise money for cancer research. Now that's really something to scream about!

▲ How About a Simple High Five?

Two baseball players learned their lessons this year about celebrating too much. You read about **Kendry Morales** of the Angels back on page 28. That accident happened in May, so you wouldn't expect to have another such event in one season, right? Wrong. In the celebration after UCLA clinched a spot in the College World Series, second baseman **Tyler Rahmatulla** ended up on the bottom of the pile. He broke his wrist and missed the World Series. Ouch!

Screeaaaaammm!

Cheering for a baseball team is one thing. Cheering for a record is another. On June 11, 50,000 fans

From Russia with Glove

The *Los Angeles Times* reported in May that until recently the Dodgers had had a very unusual employee. The team's owners had paid a man named **Vladimir Shpunt** almost as much as a backup infielder to help the team. Was Shpunt a coach? A doctor? A scout? No, he was a psychic healer. He was paid a pile of dough to sit in his room in Boston and send psychic energy flowing to Los Angeles to help the team win games. You might call this a bunch of baloney, but the Dodgers did win the N.L. West in 2008 and 2009. Are mysterious forces at work?

Octo-Soccer ▶

During the 2010 World Cup, sports fans everywhere had their eyes on an octopus. Living in a German aquarium, **Paul the Octopus** correctly selected the winners of 11 World Cup games by choosing mussels in boxes with national flags. Paul correctly picked Spain to beat his home country of Germany in the final. The Spanish president called for Paul to be protected from angry German fans who wanted to turn Paul into octopus stew!

WORLD ESKIMO-INDIAN OLYMPICS

For thousands of years, native people of the Far North have lived in the harshest conditions of cold, ice, snow, and danger. Over these years, they have developed many techniques for survival. For the past few decades, they've put those survival skills to the test . . . as sports! The World Eskimo-Indian Olympics includes events that translate the skills needed for hunting and surviving in the Arctic into games that can be held in a gym. The four man carry, for instance, comes from the strength hunters of old needed to carry home a seal. The one-foot high kick comes from an ancient way of signaling that a hunting party was returning. The Eskimo stick pull is a sort of one-on-one tug-of-war. Hunters needed great strength to yank a struggling fish from an icy hole!

The Games are now held in Fairbanks, Alaska, each year, and thousands of fans turn out to cheer for their favorites. In 2009, **Elijah Cabinboy** set a new high-kick record of 96 inches! Cheering for such performances is another way to keep warm way up North!

WEIRD CHAMPIONS

Sports is a wide, wide world of weirdness when you get away from the "traditional" sports. The superstars of the NBA, NFL, and MLB get all the headlines, but we thought some of these championship sportspeople deserved a little publicity, too. Congratulations to all these winners . . . even if you have never heard of their sports!

Lawn Mower Racing

Believe it or not, they race these things on dirt, not grass! The winners win for going fast, not cutting close.

2009 NATIONAL CHAMP: **Michael Paccione**

Mullet Tossing

A mullet is a bad, weird hairdo. But you can't toss it. A mullet is also a small fish. Now, THAT you can toss. For more than 25 years, a restaurant on the Florida-Alabama border has run the world's only interstate mullet-tossing competition. You throw the fish from one state into the other. Farthest mullet wins!

MULLET-TOSSING WORLD RECORD: **Lew Zealand**

Underwater Hockey

Okay, it's not the most fan-friendly sport, but it's pretty cool to play. Using snorkel gear and fins, players swim and push around a weighted puck with small sticks. Imagine if a hockey rink melted. . . .

2010 U.S. CHAMPION: **University of Florida** (A)

Street Luge

Lie down on a small, wheeled cart. Point your toes downhill. *Zooom!* Street luge is the road version of the super-fast ice sport. Wearing protective leathers and big helmets, lugers can reach speeds of nearly 70 miles per hour!

2009 WORLD CHAMPION: **Nick Duffield**, Australia

Concrete Canoe Racing

Engineering students from colleges around the country use their skills to make boats from concrete. Yes, that's right . . . boats made of stuff that sinks. That's where the engineering comes in.

2010 CHAMPION: **Cal Poly San Luis Obispo**

Sepak Takraw

This is basically badminton, but using your feet and a softball-sized ball made of plastic. It demands amazing agility with a soft touch. It's really popular in Asian places such as Thailand, Malaysia, and the Philippines.

2010 WORLD CHAMPION: **Thailand**

Mud Pit Belly Flopping ⏫

Part of the "Redneck Games," held in Georgia (other events include armpit noisemaking and bobbing for pigs' feet), this one is a classic: Do a big-time belly flop in a gooey pit of red-clay mud.

2010 WINNER: **Barbara Bailey** (not shown)

Camel Racing

This sport is as old as the first two desert-dwellers speeding toward an oasis. In the United States, the big race is held in the Nevada desert. Another popular event is Australia's Camel Cup, held every summer (but of course, it's winter Down Under).

2010 CAMEL CUP CHAMPION: **Dishdash**

Toe Wrestling

Held in England, this event pits competitors literally toe-to-toe. The wrestlers sit down and link big toes. They wrestle until one of them goes "toes up" or yells, "Toe much, toe much!"

2010 WINNER: **Alan Nash**

Bicycle Polo ▶▶▶

Polo is normally played while riding polo ponies. Riders use long sticks to whack a ball around a field twice as big as a football field. In bike polo, it's a rink-sized arena with three-person teams riding and whacking. And yes, they wear helmets.

2010 U.S. CHAMPION: **The Odds (Mark Capriotti, Chris Roberts,** and **Nick Vaughn)**

AMAZING KIDS*!

*Okay, two of them are in college, but they were kids just a couple of years ago! The others are teenagers, but that's close enough for this page. Meet some young people with some amazing stories.

TOP OF THE WORLD, MA! ▲

On May 21, 2010, **Jordan Romero** (center, in yellow) became the youngest person ever to reach the top of Mt. Everest. Only 13, Romero climbed with his father and several others. When he got to the top, he did what any kid would do: He called his mom! Using a satellite phone, he called back to Big Bear, California, from more than 29,000 feet above sea level. Romero left behind a lucky rabbit's foot and some seeds. He's been a climber all his life, and he aims to reach the highest peak on every continent. If he does it soon, he'll break another record. That one was set in January when Utah's **Johnny Collinson** hit the top of the seventh and final peak in that quest. He's only 17!

◀◀AROUND THE WORLD...AND NOT

In May 2010, another young person set an amazing record. Australian **Jessica Watson**, 16 (left), became the youngest person to sail alone and nonstop around the world. Her 23,000-mile journey took 210 days. She beat the "old" age record, set by 17-year-old American **Zac Sunderland** only a year earlier! Jessica steered her 34-foot (10.2 m) boat through storms and around three oceans to return to her home port of Sydney.

In June, Sunderland's sister **Abby**, also 16, tried to beat Watson's record, but a storm in the Indian Ocean knocked the mast off her boat. The world watched anxiously as rescue boats headed her way over the dark and stormy sea. But Abby was pulled from her damaged boat unharmed. A good try, but not a record.

▼ JUST SAY WOW! ▶▶

Two athletes caught the attention of the national media in the past year, not only for their talents in their respective sports, but also for the obstacles they overcame to succeed.

Anthony Robles (in white at right) was born without a right leg. So he's had his whole life to get used to that. But when he takes to the wrestling mat, an opponent has only a few seconds . . . before Robles starts

scoring point after point. Now at Arizona State, he's been an All-American twice in the 125-pound weight class and made the national finals in 2009 and 2010. He even played high school football! Robles has combined hard work and determination to succeed. "I can't even begin to tell you about the size of his heart," said his former coach **Thom Ortiz**.

Speaking of size, at 6 feet 11 inches, **Kevin Laue** has almost everything a basketball player needs. Height, strength, good footwork. He's missing just one thing: his left hand. Laue was born without that hand, but it hasn't stopped him from playing hoops since the sixth grade. His height helped, of course, but he had to learn all the basketball moves using only one hand. Today, he's a center at Manhattan College in New York City, where his hoops talent earned him a scholarship in 2009.

THE MEGA-AWESOME SPORTS INTERNET LIST!

MAJOR SPORTS WEBSITES

These are the "Big Five" of professional sports leagues. Each of these websites includes links to the individual websites of the teams in the league, plus bios of top players, video clips, schedules of games, even how to find tickets!

Major League Baseball
www.mlb.com

National Football League
www.nfl.com

National Basketball Association
www.nba.com
www.wnba.com

National Hockey League
www.nhl.com

Major League Soccer
www.mlsnet.com

Editor's Note for Parents and Teachers: These websites are for information purposes only and are not an endorsement of any program or organization over others. We've made every effort to include only websites that are appropriate for young sports fans, but the Internet is an ever-changing environment. There's no substitute for parental supervision, and we encourage everyone to surf smart . . . and safe!

OTHER SPORTS LEAGUES

Check out these websites for schedules, results, and info on athletes in your favorite sports featuring individual competitors.

Action Sports
www.asptdewtour.com

Bowling
www.pba.com

Drag Racing
www.nhra.com

Golf
www.pgatour.com
www.lpga.com

Ice Skating
www.usfigureskating.org

IndyCar Racing
www.indycar.com

**Motocross/
Supercross**
www.supercross.com

Stock Car Racing
www.nascar.com

Surfing
www.aspworldtour.com

Tennis
www.atpworldtour.com

www.sonyericsson
wtatour.com

COLLEGE SPORTS

Follow your favorite team's road to the football BCS championship or the basketball Final Four with these major college sites. You can find links to the schools that are members of these conferences.

**Bowl Championship
Series**
www.bcsfootball.org

Atlantic Coast Conference
www.theacc.com

Big East Conference
www.bigeast.org

Big Ten Conference
www.bigten.org

Big 12 Conference
www.big12sports.com

Conference USA
http://conferenceusa
.cstv.com

Mid-American Conference
www.mac-sports.com

**Mountain West
Conference**
www.themwc.com

Pac-10 Conference
www.pac-10.org

**Southeastern
Conference**
www.secsports.com

Sun Belt Conference
www.sunbeltsports.org

**Western Athletic
Conference**
www.wacsports.com

**National Collegiate
Athletic Association**
www.ncaa.com
(This site features information about all the college sports championships at every level and division.)

MAJOR SPORTS EVENTS

You'll find links to most big-time events—like the Super Bowl, the World Series, or the NBA Finals—on those sports' league websites. But here are several more world-wide sporting events that are worth a bookmark.

Little League World Series
www.littleleague.org/worldseries

The Masters
www.masters.com

Pan Am Games (2011)
www.guadalajara2011.org.mx/eng

Summer Olympics (2012)
www.london2012.com

Summer X Games
http://espn.go.com/action/xgames

Super Bowl
www.superbowl.com

Tour de France (English version)
www.letour.fr/us

Winter Olympics (2010)
www.vancouver2010.com

Winter X Games
http://espn.go.com/action/xgames

World Cup
www.fifa.com/worldcup

YOUTH SPORTS ORGANIZATIONS

Rather play than watch? These websites can help get you out on the field!

Baseball
www.littleleague.org

Basketball
www.njbl.org

Football
www.usafootball.com

Golf
www.juniorlinks.com

Ice Hockey
www.usajuniorhockey.com

Soccer
www.ayso.org

Tennis
www.usta.com

MEDIA SITES

If you're looking for the latest scores or news about your favorite sport, try some of these websites run by sports cable channels or sports publications.

CBS Sports
www.cbssports.com

ESPN
http://espn.go.com

FOX Sports
http://msn.foxsports.com

Sporting News
www.sportingnews.com

Yahoo! Sports
http://sports.yahoo.com

SPORTS HISTORY

It seems like big fans know all there is to know about the history of their favorite sports. Learn more about yours at any of these websites that take you back in time.

Hickok Sports
www.hickoksports.com

Retrosheet (Baseball)
www.retrosheet.org

Sports Illustrated **Vault**
http://vault.sportsillustrated.cnn.com/vault

Sports Reference Family of Sites
www.baseball-reference.com

www.basketball-reference.com

www.pro-football-reference.com

www.hockey-reference.com

www.sports-reference.com/olympics

PLAYERS ASSOCIATIONS

You're probably a little young to think about making money playing a sport. But if you're interested in the business side of things or want to discover more about what it's like to be a pro athlete, these sites may help.

MLB Players Association
http://mlbplayers.mlb.com

MLS Players Union
www.mlsplayers.org

NBA Players Association
www.nbpa.com

NHL Players Association
www.nhlpa.com

NFL Players Association
www.nflplayers.com

GAMES

Finally, check out these sites for some rainy-day sports fun and games on the computer.

www.nflrush.com

www.sikids.com

NCAA DIVISION I CHAMPS

MEN'S SPORTS
(2009–2010 School Year)

BC was OK in men's ice hockey.

ICE HOCKEY
Boston College

LACROSSE
Duke

RIFLE (CO-ED TEAM)
Texas Christian

SKIING (CO-ED TEAM)
Denver

SOCCER
Virginia

SWIMMING AND DIVING
Texas

BASEBALL
South Carolina

BASKETBALL
Duke

TENNIS
USC

CROSS-COUNTRY
Oklahoma State

TRACK AND FIELD (INDOOR)
Florida

FENCING (CO-ED TEAM)
Penn State

TRACK AND FIELD (OUTDOOR)
Texas A&M

FOOTBALL (BCS)
Alabama

VOLLEYBALL
Stanford

GOLF
Augusta State

WATER POLO
USC

GYMNASTICS
Michigan

WRESTLING
Iowa

WOMEN'S SPORTS
(2009–2010 School Year)

BASKETBALL
Connecticut

BOWLING
Fairleigh Dickinson

CROSS-COUNTRY
Villanova

FIELD HOCKEY
North Carolina

GOLF
Purdue

GYMNASTICS
UCLA

LACROSSE
Maryland

ICE HOCKEY
Minnesota Duluth

ROWING
Virginia

SOCCER
North Carolina

SOFTBALL
UCLA

SWIMMING AND DIVING
Florida

TENNIS
Stanford

TRACK AND FIELD (INDOOR)
Oregon

TRACK AND FIELD (OUTDOOR)
Texas A&M

VOLLEYBALL
Penn State

WATER POLO
USC

Maryland's women's lacrosse team came from behind late to win the national title.

THE BIG EVENTS CALENDAR

September 2010

5 Cycling
Mountain Bike World
Championships, final day,
Beaupré, Quebec, Canada

6–10 Wrestling
World Championships,
Moscow, Russia

9 Pro Football
Regular season begins

Mountain bikers go for the gold!

13–27 Weightlifting
World Championships,
Turkey

19–26 Gymnastics
World Rhythmic Gymnastics
Championships, Moscow, Russia

23–26 Golf
PGA Tour Championship,
Atlanta, Georgia

25–26 Tennis
U.S. Open finals,
New York City

TBA* Basketball
WNBA Finals

October 2010

1–3 Golf
Ryder Cup, Newport, Wales

6 Baseball
MLB play-offs begin

9 Track
Ironman Triathlon World
Championship, Kona, Hawaii

TBA* Baseball
MLB League Championship
Series begin

16–24 Gymnastics
World Artistic Gymnastics
Championships,
Rotterdam, Netherlands

27 Baseball
World Series begins

Meb Keflezighi won the 2009 New York City Marathon: 26 miles in just over two hours!

November 2010

7 Running
New York City Marathon

21 NASCAR
Ford 400, Homestead, Florida
(final race of Chase for the Cup)

21 Soccer
MLS Cup,
Toronto, Ontario, Canada

December 2010

4 College Football
ACC Championship,
Tampa, Florida
SEC Championship,
Atlanta, Georgia

Big 12 Championship,
Arlington, Texas

5 College Soccer
Women's championship game,
Raleigh, North Carolina

12 College Soccer
Men's championship game,
Santa Barbara, California

January 2011

1 College Football
Rose Bowl, Pasadena, California
Fiesta Bowl, Glendale, Arizona

3 College Football
FedEx Orange Bowl,
Miami, Florida

Pairs skaters Caydee Denney and Jeremy Barrett compete in the 2009 nationals.

4 College Football
Sugar Bowl,
New Orleans, Louisiana

8–9 Pro Football
Wild-Card Play-off Weekend

11 College Football
Bowl Championship Series
National Championship Game,
Glendale, Arizona

15–16 Pro Football
Divisional Play-off Weekend

17–30 Tennis
Australian Open,
Melbourne

22–30 Figure Skating
U.S. Figure Skating
Championships,
Greensboro, North Carolina

23 Pro Football
Conference Championships

27–30 Action Sports
Winter X Games, Aspen,
Colorado

February 2011

6 Pro Football
Super Bowl XLV, Cowboys
Stadium, Arlington, Texas

20 NASCAR
Daytona 500,
Daytona Beach, Florida

20 Pro Basketball
NBA All-Star Game,
Los Angeles, California

March 2011

21–27 Figure Skating
World Figure Skating
Championships, Tokyo, Japan

April 2011

2–5 Basketball
NCAA Men's and Women's
Final Four, Houston, Texas, and
Indianapolis, Indiana

7–10 Golf
The Masters, Augusta, Georgia

May 2011

7 Horse Racing
Kentucky Derby, Churchill
Downs, Louisville, Kentucky

21 Horse Racing
Preakness Stakes, Pimlico
Race Course, Baltimore,
Maryland

29 Auto Racing
Indianapolis 500,
Indianapolis, Indiana

June 2011

4–5 Tennis
French Open, final matches,
Paris

11 Horse Racing
Belmont Stakes, Belmont Park,
Elmont, New York

TBA* Hockey
Stanley Cup championship
series begins

TBA* Basketball
NBA Finals begin

16–19 Golf
U.S. Open Championship,
Bethesda, Maryland

18 College Baseball
College World Series,
Omaha, Nebraska

19 Tennis
All-England Championships at
Wimbledon begin

July 2011

2 Cycling
Tour de France begins,
Passage du Gois, France

7–10 Golf
U.S. Women's Open,
Colorado Springs, Colorado

12 Baseball
MLB All-Star Game,
Phoenix, Arizona

14–17 Golf
British Open Championship,
Sandwich, Kent, England

TBA* Action Sports
Summer X Games, site TBA

August 2011

TBA* Golf
LPGA Championship

TBA* Baseball
Little League World Series

11–14 Golf
PGA Championship,
Johns Creek, Georgia

*TBA: To be announced. Actual dates of event not available at press time.

Produced by Shoreline Publishing Group LLC

Santa Barbara, California

www.shorelinepublishing.com

President/Editorial Director: James Buckley, Jr.

Designed by Tom Carling, www.carlingdesign.com

The *Year in Sports* text was written by

James Buckley, Jr., & Jim Gigliotti

plus **Beth Adelman** (NHL) and **Ellen Labrecque** (NBA).

Thanks to Brenda Murray, Stephanie Anderson, Chris Hernandez, Steven Scott, and the all-stars at Scholastic for all their extra-inning and overtime help!

Photo research was done by the authors. Thanks to Dwayne Howard of Scholastic Picture Services for his assistance in obtaining the photos.

● ●

$9.99 US / $12.99 CAN

YEAR IN SPORTS 2011

The *Scholastic Year in Sports* gives you an in-depth look at all of the hottest stars and most memorable moments from the past sports season. Relive the drama, the excitement, and the victories—plus a few of the losses!

DO YOU REMEMBER THESE INCREDIBLE EVENTS?

★ The New Orleans Saints' stunning Super Bowl win

★ Shaun White's awesome gold-medal snowboarding shred

★ Two perfect games in baseball—in the same month

★ The drama of soccer's World Cup

All those stories, along with stats, records, stars, and more, are inside, plus sneak peeks at big sports news in the year ahead. The *Scholastic Year in Sports* is a must-have for every sports fan . . . and fans of every sport!

SCHOLASTIC
www.scholastic.com

ISBN 978-0-545-23749-9

50999

EAN

9 780545 237499